SOFT-EDGE PIECING

JINNY BEYER

SOFT-EDGE PIECING

JINNY BEYER

*Add the elegance of appliqué
to traditional-style patchwork design*

C&T PUBLISHING

© 1995 Jinny Beyer

Photography by Sharon Risedorph, San Francisco.
Diagrams and illustrations by Jinny Beyer.
Editing by Louise Owens Townsend.
Technical editing by Joyce Engels Lytle.
Book design by Kajun Graphics, San Francisco.
Cover design by Jinny Beyer and Kajun Graphics.

Published by C&T Publishing, P.O. Box 1456, Lafayette, California 94549.

ISBN 0-914881-94-9

All rights reserved. No part of this work covered by the copyright hereon may be reproduced or used in any form or by any means—graphic, electronic, or mechanical, including photocopying, recording, taping, or information storage and retrieval systems—without written permission of the publisher. Copyrights on individual works are retained by the artists as noted in *Soft-Edge Piecing*.

Library of Congress Cataloging-in-Publication Data

Beyer, Jinny
    Soft-edge piecing : add the elegance of appliqué to traditional style patchwork / Jinny Beyer. — 1st ed.
       p.   cm.
    Includes bibliographical references (p. 144).
    ISBN 0-914881-94-9
    1. Patchwork — Patterns.   2. Quilting — Patterns.   3. Appliqué — Patterns   I. Title.
TT835.B46 1995
746.46—dc20   94–38483
                                             CIP

Dritz Fray Check is a trademark of the Sewing Notions Division of Risdon Corporation.
Quilter's Disk is a product of Dritz Corporation.
Triangle Tailor's Chalk is a product of Clover Needlecraft, Inc.

Printed in Hong Kong
First Edition

10   9   8   7   6   5   4   3   2

CONTENTS

ACKNOWLEDGMENTS

Once again a special recognition to my husband John who lives through a lot of chaos during any book project. A thank you to C&T Publishing for giving me the opportunity to work with them on this book, and to Hans Andress, textile artist, whose fine hand and intuitive interpretation created the beautiful fabric designs found on almost every page of this book. My thanks to the women who helped me develop the soft-edge technique into a seminar theme, some of whose quilts are also pictured here: Darlene Christopherson, Kathryn Kuhn, Fay Goldey, Nancy Johnson, Kay Lettau, Lenore Parham, Linda Pool, Jay Moody, Gayle Ropp, Yoko Sawanobori, Judy Spahn, Bonnie Stratton, and Ellen Swanson. To Jill Johnson, textile artist; Dan Ramsey, graphic artist; Sharon Risedorph, photographer; Louise Townsend, editor, and Joyce Lytle, technical editor; and to quiltmakers Cindy Blackberg, Janine Holzman, Marjorie Lydecker, and Margaret Smith for their beautiful work. To Robin Morrison who helped me get it all together, and to David Adamson who taught me to use my computer to the best advantage. And finally thanks to MAC for helping me with the illustrations.

INTRODUCTION

Years ago someone said to me, "Now that you have explored the use of borders and medallion quilts, what is going to be the thrust of your work in the future?" I was a little taken aback by that question because I have never *planned* what I was going to do in the future. I work on whatever idea appeals to me at the time. My philosophy has always been to follow my heart, to do what seems right at the moment, and the ideas will come. If I force myself to try to come up with a new idea, the result can be stilted and lack spontaneity.

It is interesting how new ideas do develop, at least for me. It is sort of like shopping for clothes. When shopping for a specific type of garment for a particular occasion, I can never find just what I need; yet when I'm not looking for anything and don't even have time for shopping, perfect items seem to jump out at me. Likewise, if someone tells me to come up with a new way to create quilts, I can struggle and struggle and seem to face a blank wall; yet very often while designing a quilt, diverse ideas that I have been working on for years come together and spark an entirely new concept.

Soft-edge piecing came about in just such a way. Becoming quite frustrated while working on a new quilt, I searched in vain for the perfect fabric to fit into a certain shape. Finally, one day I found a new paisley design that had all the right colors. However, the pattern on the fabric was so beautiful that it seemed a shame to cut it up to fit the shape as that would spoil the overall flow of the fabric design itself.

As I balked at cutting into the fabric, the idea of "soft-edge piecing" suddenly came to me. The concept was an entirely new way to look at geometric shapes, yet an outgrowth of all the years I had worked with border prints and cut them up to add special touches to geometric patchwork designs. I used the technique in the quilt I was working on, and that lead to even more ideas. The group of us that work together each year planning my annual Hilton Head Seminar decided to develop the idea further and use it as a theme for the following year's seminar. As a result, many beautiful quilts have been made, some of which are pictured on these pages. As we worked on our quilts, it seemed natural to call the technique "soft-edge piecing."

This book will take you step-by-step through the process of creating your own soft-edge block or quilt, in much the same way as I learned and developed the technique. The information is presented in the same way as my classes on the subject are taught. There are numerous illustrations and instructions explaining first the use of border prints (repeat-striped fabrics in which the stripes can be cut apart and used to outline or frame shapes, blocks, and quilts) and then both border prints and other fabrics to create "soft-edge" blocks. If you have a basic knowledge of the use of border prints, it will be much easier to go the next step to the soft edge. A series of exercises have been laid out to help both the student and teacher gain an understanding of the concept. It is one thing to look at the illustrations and see the effect that the use of these fabrics has on a design, but it is another to actually have the experience of doing it yourself. The exercises can be used in classroom settings by teachers, or by individuals reading this book on their own.

Twenty new quilt block designs are also included for you to try the soft-edge technique. These never-before-published designs are some of the original patterns that I have developed during the past four years. Five of them are given as full-sized patterns, and guides for drafting the others are found in Chapter 5, along with piecing and construction techniques. Follow the exercises, experiment with the new designs and patterns given here, and then have fun applying this exciting new concept to your favorite quilt block.

Chapter 1

PRELIMINARY TO SOFT-EDGE PIECING: WORKING WITH BORDER PRINTS

n order for you to understand the concept of working with prints to create soft edges, it is helpful for you to begin as I did, by first working with border prints, and to understand how kaleidoscopic and unusual effects can be created by mirror-imaging motifs, and by repeating shapes cut from identical places on the fabric. Once you have had some experience, it will be easier to go the next step to the soft edge.

For years I have enjoyed the challenge of looking at a patchwork block and figuring out where in that block a border print could be added. The most common shape to work with is a square. Look at the line drawing and then colored version of *Swamp Patch* (shown below in Illustrations 1–1 and 1–2). If the block has a large square in the center, such as this design, I will invariably divide the square diagonally from corner to corner, creating four triangles (1–3).

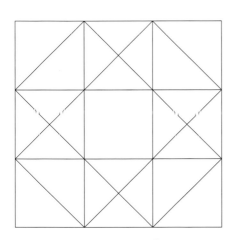

1–1. Swamp Patch

1–2

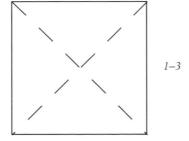

1–3

I make a template from one of the triangles and then cut four identical triangles from a border print. One of the aspects of working with border prints that I particularly like is the fact that the various shapes can be outlined using a small stripe from the print. Therefore, when cutting out the pieces, I like to place the template with the long side of the triangle on the straight grain of the fabric along a line on the border print so the square will be "framed" (1–4). The triangles are then sewn together to once again form a square, as in the center of *Swamp Patch* shown below (1–5 and 1–6).

1–4

1–5

1–6

The square can also be cut into four smaller squares with each piece cut identically but centered *diagonally* on the print. Those squares can then be sewn back together to once more form the larger square. When cutting the squares in this way, there will be no border or "outline" around the outside of the square. Therefore, I like to make the finished "square" slightly smaller and then frame it with a small border around the outer edge.

The illustrations here show the square divided into four smaller squares (1–7), then a template made from one of those squares placed diagonally on the fabric (1–8), four of those squares put together (1–9),

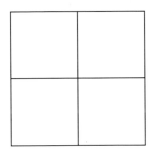

1–7

1–8

1–9

1–10

and finally what that square looks like with a small border added around the edges (1–10).

Many times a border print can be used in more than one place within the block. Look at *Swamp Patch* again and see if there are other places where a border print might be effective. I have added a border print to the triangles in the corners as shown in Illustration 1–11. Note that the triangles have been cut so that once again there is a small line "outlining" the long edge of the triangle.

Octagons form the centers of many designs, and octagons broken into eight triangles create a perfect opportunity for using border prints. Once again all the triangles are cut from identical places on the fabric, and

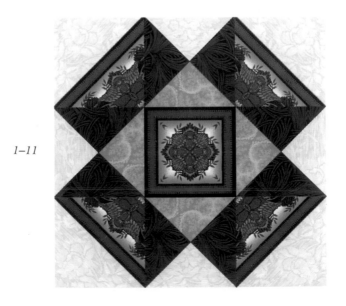

1–11

when they are sewn together, an exciting design unfolds. Many different variations can be made from the same border print, depending on where the pieces are cut.

The traditional *Rolling Star* block in Illustration 1–12 has been altered so that each of the diamonds forming the center star has been divided in half sideways and now contains two triangles. The eight triangles at the center of the block form an octagon.

The illustrations below show the *Rolling Star* block with a "border print" octagon in the center (1–13), the stripe from which the octagon was cut (1–14), and, on the next page, six additional octagons cut from

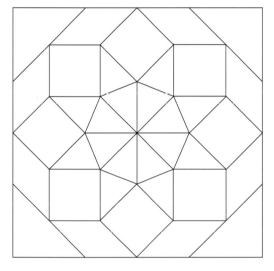

1–12
Rolling Star

1–13

1–14

1–15

the *same* border, but from different places on that border (1–15). It is amazing how many different effects can be achieved from just one border-print fabric.

Border prints can be used effectively in other shapes as well. Another one I enjoy working with is a diamond. Two possible ways of dividing a diamond are shown in Illustration 1–16. Once again, to be effective, the pieces must be cut identically from the same place on the fabric, but now the motifs must be *mirror-imaged*. Please note the arrows on each illustration. They indicate where I like to place both the straight grain of the fabric as well as a "line" from the border stripe.

➥ N O T E : *In order for this to work, you must use a fabric that contains mirror-image motifs.*

The diamond on the top is broken into two triangles. When cutting the pieces, you will cut one piece, then *flip* the template (mirror-image it), and cut the other piece, as an exact mirror image of the first.

The second diamond is made from *four* smaller triangles. Two triangles are cut identically; the other two are also cut identically but are mirror images of the first two.

Notice illustrations 1–17 and 1–18 below where the same *Rolling Star* block shown on page 13 is used, but now these two diamond variations are added in part of the design. A third variation is shown in Illustration 1–19 where the entire diamond is cut from a single piece of border print.

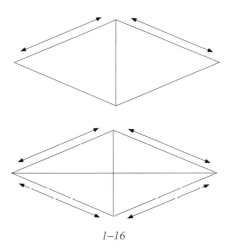

1–16

1–17

1–18

1–19

➥ N O T E : *Use a transparent template material. It will be much easier to center motifs and cut identical pieces if you can see through your template material. After cutting one piece, mark part of the design from the fabric directly onto the template. This will be a guide for placing the template on the fabric again and will aid in getting the next pieces cut accurately.*

Almost any shape can be changed to accommodate the use of border prints, often drastically altering the appearance of a design. The same *Rolling Star* block on pages 13 and 15 is shown in two more illustrations below, where the border print has been used in even different ways.

1–20

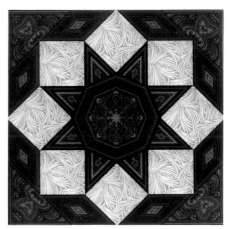

1–21

PHOTOCOPYING FABRICS

It is often impossible to find more of a certain fabric in the middle of a project. Therefore most people are reluctant to cut up their fabrics without knowing what the end result is going to look like. For all quilting projects, the photocopy machine is an invaluable tool. Fabric can be placed directly on the copy machine and duplicated. If the image is poor, try a different brand machine. My experience is that some machines copy fabrics better than others. Most self-service copy houses have more than one type of machine, so experiment until you find the one that does the best job. If you have the same print in different color combinations, copy the print with the most contrast in the colors.

Many copy machines have a standard 64% reduction. In order to save paper, reduce the fabric to the maximum allowed on the machine. Then reduce the patchwork block by the same amount so that you will know how the fabric will look in the size block you are planning to use. Avoid photocopying from another copy as each generation will be less clear than the last, and some machines distort the image slightly.

The copies of border print fabrics shown on pages 19–20 have both been reduced by 64% of actual size. The block designs for experimental use have also been reduced. The blocks shown here for the exercises are 7", which is approximately 64% of an 11" block.

➥ NOTE: *Use a red marker. When working with photocopies, it will be easier to see where you have marked if you use a red marker for drawing around templates. Black markers blend in too much with the photocopy. When working with black-and-white photocopies, in order to see better, it is also helpful to mark the design on your template with a permanent red marker.*

USING MIRRORS

Even when cutting paper, I find students are reluctant to cut into the paper without knowing what the end result will be. A set of mirrors can be very useful when planning how to cut out both the paper and the actual fabric. Pocket mirrors with no frame, a set of locker mirrors (with square edges), or even mirrored bathroom tiles work well. Or check your local quilt shop for mirrors packaged specifically for quilters.

Place the template on the fabric or paper in the place you are thinking about cutting. If the template has added seam allowances, gently place the mirrors on top of the template directly on the seam allowance. If the seam allowance has not been added, put the mirrors along the sides of the template. In any event the edges of the mirrors should come together at the *angle* where all of the pieces in the shape will come together when sewn. Carefully pull the template away without disturbing the position or angle of the mirrors. Look directly into the mirrors and you will see what the fabric will look like if multiple pieces are cut from the same spot and then sewn together.

➥ NOTE: *Working with two mirrors can become a bit awkward. You may find it easier to tape the mirrors together. Put mirror sides facing each other, and tape one side of the two mirrors together using a wide tape. The mirrors will then open and close like a book, and you can easily open them to any angle you want.*

Even though the explanation of using borders within different shapes may seem straightforward, you will learn much more if you actually create some shapes yourself. The following exercises give step-by-step instructions for using borders within various shapes. I urge you to do each of the exercises, experimenting with several different fabrics and variations, as this will give you the experience of designing with borders and will make the transition to the "soft edge" much easier.

WORKING WITH BORDER PRINTS IN INDIVIDUAL SHAPES

For this series of exercises you will need:

• Some geometric shapes (draw your own, or photocopy or trace the shapes on this page)

• Photocopies of border print fabric (use your own or photocopy one of the fabrics on the next two pages)

• Transparent template plastic

• Red or black permanent marker

• Paper-cutting scissors

• 6″ ruler

• Small right-angle (90°) triangle

• Glue

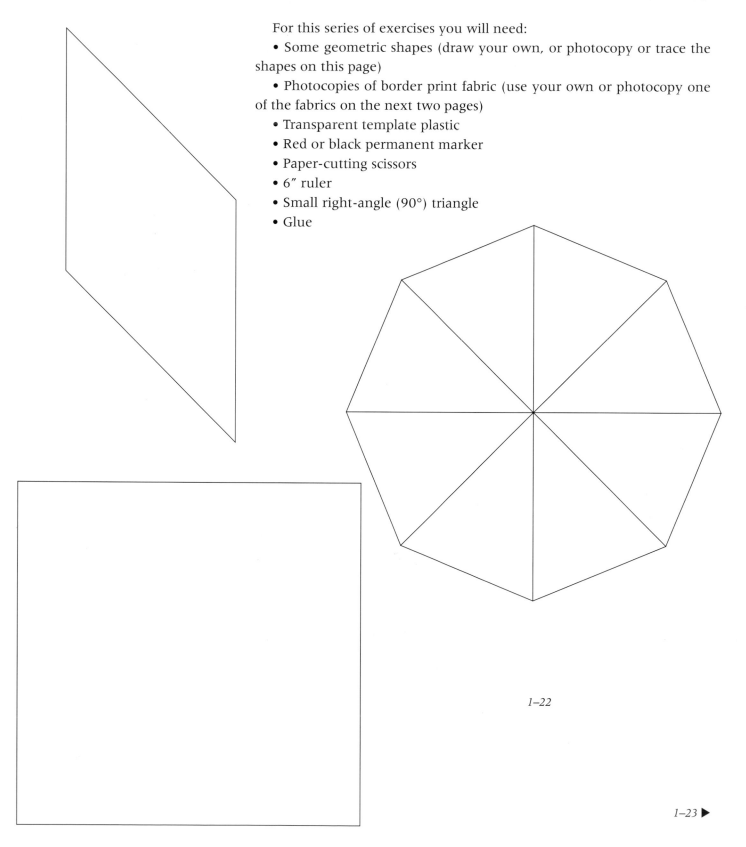

1–22

1–23 ▶

Squares

METHOD 1

Step 1. Begin with the square shown on page 18 in Illustration 1–22. Create four triangles by drawing straight lines from corner to corner in both directions (1–25), then make a plastic template from one of the triangles (1–26). As you will be working in paper, do not worry about adding seam allowance.

Step 2. In order to accurately center the template on the fabric, you will need a line dividing the template in half. Put the right-angle triangle on top of the template with one side lined up along the bottom of the template and the other side meeting at the point as shown in Illustration 1–27 below. Draw a line down the center of the template.

Step 3. Place the triangle template over the photocopy of the border print with the long side of the triangle along what would be the straight grain of the fabric. Try to get some line from the fabric to fall just inside the template. Next, using the line dividing the template in half as a reference point, center some motif from the stripe in the middle of the template as shown in Illustration 1–28 on the next page.

My experience is that no matter where you put the template, as long as the four triangles are cut identically, the result will always look good. Therefore, I don't bother with the mirrors, but just wait to be surprised at how the design looks when the shapes are all put together. But if you want to know ahead of time, this is when you should get out the mirrors for a preview.

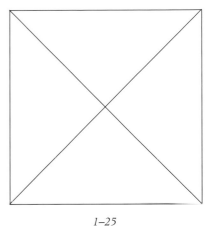

1–25

1–26

◀ 1–24

1–27

1–28

1–29

After you have centered the triangle template on the photocopy, place the mirrors along its two short edges, so that the sides of the mirrors meet at the right angle. Carefully remove the template without disturbing the mirrors, and look into them to see what four identical triangles would look like. If you like what you see, place the template back onto the border print.

Step 4. Using the permanent marker, draw some part of the design from the fabric directly onto the template. This will be a reference point. Draw around the template (you will be able to see a red pen line easier than a black one), and cut the triangle out. Then draw and cut three more triangles identical to the first, using the reference point marked on the template as a guide.

Step 5. Form a square of the four triangles and glue them to a piece of paper (1–29).

➥ N O T E : *For these exercises you are working with paper and gluing the results to another piece of paper. When you transfer these ideas to fabric you will have to add the seam allowance to the template and take into account how to cut the fabric to allow for that seam.*

METHOD 2

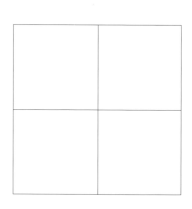

1–30

Step 1. Divide the square this time into four squares instead of triangles by finding the midpoint on all of the sides and connecting the midpoints. Make a template from one of the smaller squares (1–30).

Step 2. Draw a line on the template directly down the middle by connecting one corner to its opposite corner. This line will be used as a guide for evenly centering the template on the fabric (1–30).

Step 3. Place the template *diagonally* on the fabric, and move it around until you find a motif you would like to use. Make sure that the diagonal line is centered on a mirror-imaged motif in the fabric. Mark around the template and, before removing it, remember to mark part of the fabric motif directly onto the template so that you will have a guide for marking the remaining squares (1–31).

Step 4. Cut out the square.

Step 5. Cut three more pieces identical to the first and glue them to a piece of paper (1–32).

1–32

1–31

Step 6. If you want to have an outline around the square as in Illustration 1–35, cut a small stripe from the border print and apply it around all four sides. If this was going to be done in actual fabric and the square was part of the patchwork design, you would have to remake the templates and cut a separate template for the "outline."

In other words, when working with a specific-size block, the size of the final square should not change. If you want to add an outline to the square, you will have to make the actual square *smaller* so that when the outline is added, it will still be the proper size. If the finished square is 3", and the outline is $1/4$", then measure $1/4$" in from all sides of the square and draw a line for the outline (1–33). Divide the square into four smaller squares and make a a template for both the small square and the outline strip (1–34). If you are doing this in fabric, add the seam allowance around all sides of both pieces.

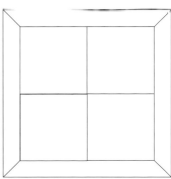

1–33

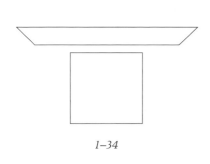

1–34

1–35

Octagons

Now try an octagon. Making the octagon is identical to making the square in Exercise 1, Method 1 on pages 21–22. The only difference is that you will now be working with a differently shaped triangle template and will be cutting eight identical triangles instead of four.

Step 1. Make a template from one of the eight triangles, which form the octagon on page 18.

Step 2. Using the right-angle triangle as in Squares, Method 1, Step 2 on page 21, draw a line down the middle of the template (1–36).

Step 3. Place the triangle on the border print so that the *short* side falls along a line in the border print, centering the template on some motif in the fabric (1–37). If you want to see what the design will look like, use the mirrors as described on page 17.

Step 4. Cut eight identical triangles and glue them to a piece of paper (1–38).

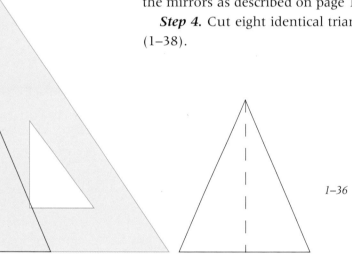

1–36

1–37

1–38

Triangles

Triangles similar to the one used in the octagon on page 24, are often part of patchwork designs as in the *Rolling Star* blocks shown here and on pages 13, 15, and 16. When I encounter a design of this sort, I will often "chevron" the border print as shown in Blocks 1–20 and 1–21 on page 16. To do this:

Step 1. With the right-angle triangle as an aid, divide the triangle exactly in half, (see Squares, Method 1, Step 2 on page 21), then make a template the size of one of the halves (1–40).

Step 2. Put an arrow directly on the template along the *longest* edge. This arrow indicates where the straight grain of the fabric should go (1–40).

Step 3. Place the template on the border print photocopy with the longest part of the triangle along the straight grain of the fabric—I like to include a small stripe from the border along that long edge (1–41). Move the template around until you find an area you would like to incorporate into the design.

Step 4. When you are satisfied with the motif you have centered, draw a portion of the design directly on the template, then draw around the template with a red marker.

Step 5. Next, carefully flip (mirror-image) the template and, using the mark that was drawn onto the template as a guide, line it up on the border print in exactly the same part of the design as on the previous piece, and draw the second triangle (1–41). Cut the two triangles out. When they are put together they will create a chevron effect (1–42) .

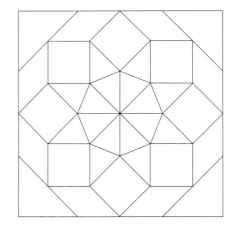

1–39
Rolling Star

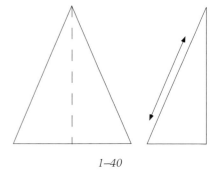

1–40

1–41

1–42

Diamonds

When I'm planning to use a border print, there are two ways in which I like to divide diamonds.

METHOD 1

The first method involves dividing the diamond in half both lengthwise and sideways, as in Illustration 1–43. Please note that this is simply two of the previous triangles in Illustration 1–40, put together. Once again it is more effective if the outer edge of the diamond has a small stripe from the border as an "outline."

Steps 1–2. Cut the pieces exactly the same as for the triangle in Illustration 1–40, but instead of cutting two pieces, cut four. Note that in the illustration, the triangles marked with an **O** will be cut exactly the same, and the ones marked with an **X** are mirror images of the first (1–44 to 1–46).

Even if you did the previous triangle, make a diamond for practice using a different fabric or cut from a different place on the fabric. It can be somewhat confusing when mirror-imaging motifs, and this practice will help you to understand better if you try at least one. To see what one of these diamonds will look like before cutting the fabric, place the template on the fabric with the *long* edge along the straight grain. Put the two mirrors on the shortest sides of the triangle with the edges of the mirror meeting at the right angle. Carefully remove the template and look into the mirrors to see what the diamond will look like.

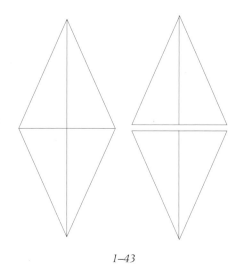

1–43

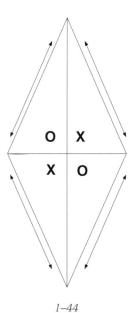

1–44

1–45

1–46

METHOD 2

Step 1. The second method involves dividing the diamond in half sideways only. If you have made a triangle template for the octagon on page 18, you can use that. Otherwise, divide the diamond shape (page 18) in half sideways as in Illustration 1–47. The arrows indicate where the straight grain of the fabric will go.

Step 2. Place the template on the fabric with a line from the fabric along one of the *long* edges of the template (this is where the arrow is). To see what the design will look like before cutting the pieces, use a single mirror. Put the mirror on the short edge of the template.

Step 3. If you are satisfied with what you see in the mirrors, mark part of the design from the fabric directly onto the template, draw around the template on the fabric, and cut out the first triangle.

Step 4. Carefully flip (mirror-image) the template and, using the marking on the template as a guide, align the template on the border print centering the same image as the previous piece and mark, then cut out the second triangle (1–48).

Step 5. Paste the two triangles next to each other on a piece of paper (1–49). Also refer to Illustration 1–17 on page 15 to see what this motif looks like in a completed block.

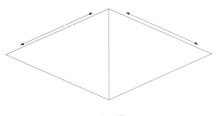

1–47

1–48

1–49

Working With Border Prints in Patchwork Design

Now that you have had some experience in working with borders in individual shapes, it is time to try putting borders in a complete design. It is good to keep in mind that you will be using *other* fabrics as well as the borders. A design composed of all border prints could be overwhelming.

In addition to the items listed on page 18, you will also need:

• A line drawing of a patchwork block, approximately 7" in size. (Choose one of your own, or copy one of the ones in Illustrations 1–50 and 1–51 on pages 29–30, or 4-35 and 4–36 on pages 80–81.)

• A photocopy of one of the border prints on pages 19–20 or photocopy your own fabric at a 64% reduction.

Step 1. Refer to the *Rolling Star* illustrations on pages 13, 15, and 16, and look again at how many different ways the border print has been used in each of those illustrations. Now look at your own design and try to find places to use a border print. You may find shapes not previously illustrated here, but by now you should be able to see how the border could be used.

Step 2. Divide each shape into however many pieces you need for the variation you plan on doing. Make the templates for each shape. Follow the steps listed previously for cutting the border prints and have fun!

Step 3. Do the design at least two different ways so that you can see how different it can look, depending on where the border print is used.

1–50
Atlantic Jewel

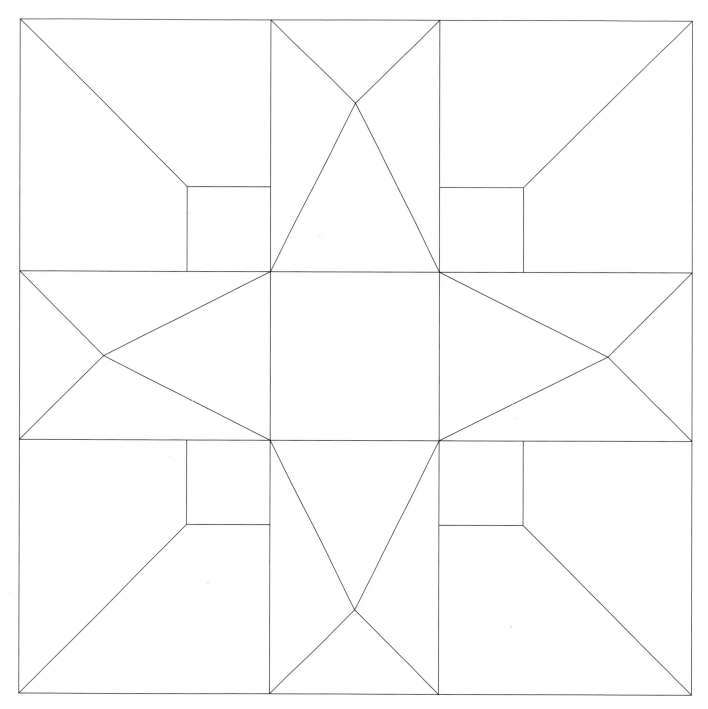

1–51
La Mancha

Chapter 2

DISCOVERING SOFT-EDGE PIECING

The idea for soft-edge piecing came about, as mentioned briefly earlier, because I had been searching for an answer to a dilemma in a quilting project. While working on a *Mariner's Compass* quilt following my usual procedure, I had made a black-and-white drawing of the blocks and had shaded them according to the light, medium, and dark placement of the colors. My original idea was to find a large-print, multi-colored fabric, which coordinated with the colors in the blocks and could be inserted into the spaces between the compasses (similar to the drawing in Illustration 2–1).

2–1

2–2

I searched in vain for the perfect fabric, and was becoming quite frustrated when one day I found a new fabric design. It was the paisley print shown in Illustration 2–2.

That fabric had all of the right colors and seemed to be a good choice for the quilt, but the more I looked at it, the harder it was for me to cut up the print. It seemed that cutting the fabric up to fit the motif between the compasses, would spoil the overall flow of the fabric design itself.

As I balked at cutting up the fabric, an idea suddenly came to me. It seemed that with geometric patchwork blocks, we *always* cut the fabric to fit within the individual shapes. Thus, the geometry of the design dictates how a fabric is used, and very often a beautiful part of the fabric is spoiled because it has to be cut apart to fit into the shape. So why not, for once, let the print on the fabric dictate the boundaries of the geometric design? I began experimenting with ways to cut the paisley fabric apart following its pattern and allowing the design to extend beyond the boundaries of the shape.

For years I have been working with border prints, finding places within a patchwork block to use that type of print, just as you have done in the previous chapter. With this experience as background, I decided to cut the paisley in a similar way. Beginning with a square, I divided it into fourths, realizing those quarter sections would eventually be sewn back together again. (See Illustration 2–3a. The dashed line indicates where the smaller squares will be joined to once again form a larger shape.) I took one of those quarter sections, made a template, centered it over one of the motifs in the paisley fabric, then cut along the two sides of the

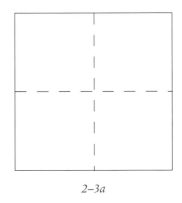

2–3a

2–3b

2–3c

2–4

template where the blocks would be rejoined, but cut *beyond* the boundaries of the square on the other two sides, following the design in the fabric (2–3b). I drew the design of the fabric directly onto the template to make it easier to match the same place on the fabric when cutting three more identical pieces (2–3c).

After sewing the four pieces together and placing the motif between the compasses, I realized that there ought to be something *darke*r in the design as well. So I found a darker paisley fabric and created a teardrop by mirror imaging a part of one of the paisleys as shown in Illustration 2–4. That teardrop was tucked under the edges of the other design, and the completed motif was then appliquéd to the quilt top. I later decided the quilt needed another very dark accent, so I appliquéd a dark "curved square" in the middle of each paisley motif. The resulting design is shown below. Prior to quilting, the extra fabric was cut away from *behind* the appliqué to eliminate the extra layer and to facilitate the quilting. It was so exciting to see the effect of the appliqué motifs between the compasses that I decided to use a similar technique for the border.

After completing the quilt top shown on the facing page, I became very intrigued about the possibilities of transferring what I had done as a

P2–1. Detail of soft-edge motif between Mariner's Compass *blocks on quilt top made by author.*

P2–2. Mariner's Compass *quilt top, made by the author, was the first inspiration for the soft-edge piecing technique.*

setting motif in my quilt to actual geometric patchwork designs. The idea of combining both piecing and appliqué in the same block, of allowing the curved lines of the appliqué to add a softness to the hard line geometry was very intriguing. Very few traditional quilt designs combine both piecing and appliqué (*Fan, Lily, Baskets*, and *Dresden Plate* come to mind), and even if they do, the appliqué part is rarely cut to follow an actual design on the fabric. What I wanted to try was to let an interesting fabric still give the illusion of the geometric shape it was replacing, but to let the *fabric* dictate the boundaries of that shape. I found myself looking at fabrics in a completely new way, seeing which ones had edges in the designs that would lend themselves to appliqué. In fact I found myself using a term that I don't think is in the English language. I was searching for fabrics with "appliquéable" edges, ones that had soft curves with thicker lines delineating the motifs.

It was great fun experimenting with some very traditional patchwork designs, looking at fabric in new ways, and discovering ways in which parts of the design could be altered to create a "soft edge." Some examples of those experiments follow. Look at the *Swamp Patch* block shown again here in the traditional way I might make it using border prints (2–5). The squares in the corners of the block are composed of two triangles. But let's look at how you would go about creating a "soft edge" in the corners. Instead of cutting two separate triangles, one larger square template is made from which the background fabric will be cut. Then a line is drawn diagonally from corner to corner of the square to aid in centering (2–6a). Now the *same* template is placed on a fabric containing areas that can be used for a soft edge. The idea is still to give the

2–5. Swamp Patch

illusion of a triangle in the corner of the block, but for that triangle to have a curved or "soft" edge. The square template is placed in various spots on the fabric until a suitable place to cut from is found. Now the fabric will be *cut to the template* in the places where it will be *pieced* and *cut following the design on the fabric* in the places where it will be *appliquéd*. Therefore, along the seam lines the standard 1/4" is cut, and along the appliqué or *soft* parts, a narrower 1/8" is cut to allow for turning under the appliqué. The heavy black line in Illustration 2–6b indicates the *finished* motif. The white line indicates where the piece is cut including seam allowances.

➥ N O T E : *This is the only time the seam allowance will be designated in the illustrations.*

After the background and soft pieces are cut, the soft motif is carefully placed on the background fabric, basted in place, and then appliquéd down (2–6c).

➥ N O T E : *Before the square is sewn into the design, the excess fabric is cut away from behind the appliqué to eliminate the two thicknesses of fabric.*

At this time, the completed square is treated as any other part of the block and is pieced into the design in the normal fashion. Compare the differences in the traditional version of *Swamp Patch* on the previous page and the soft-edge version (2–7).

It is amazing to see the differences that occur between the hard-line traditional blocks and their soft-edge counterparts. The softness lends a nice balance to the overall design and interrupts the hard-line geometry. Furthermore, even though the soft-edge technique looks complicated, it is really no more difficult than the traditional way of piecing, and simpler

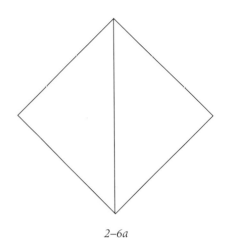

2–6a

2–6b

2–6c

2–7

blocks lend themselves better to the technique than more complex ones.

Another block, *Atlantic Jewel* (2–8), is illustrated below in my traditional method of working with a border print within a design. In that pattern, there are small points appearing to come from behind the larger ones. Each of those points has a background fabric on either side (2–9).

To change those points to a soft edge, one larger background template the size of the point *plus* the two pieces on either side of the point would be made. The background fabric would be cut from that larger template and then the same template would be used for the soft-edge pieces. The soft-edge fabric would be *cut to the template* in the places where it will be

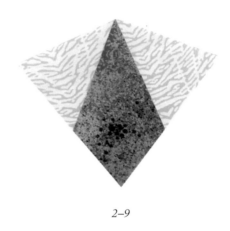

2–9

2–8. Atlantic Jewel

2–10

2–11

pieced into the block and *to the fabric design* in the places where it would be appliquéd, allowing, of course, enough extra to turn under for sewing.

The border print fabric that was chosen to be used for the soft-edge variation is shown in Illustration 2–10. That particular fabric has wonderful soft-edge possibilities because of the smooth curved edges. A red line indicates the part of the fabric that was cut for the soft-edge technique. The completed soft-edge variation of *Atlantic Jewel* is shown in Illustration 2–11. It is amazing how completely different the design looks with only that one change from Illustration 2–8.

A border print has been used in three different places in the *Spring House* variation shown in Illustration 2–12.

Two additional shapes have been altered using the soft-edge technique in the following illustrations. First, the small squares next to the center star have been changed. In this case there is a small square with two small "background" triangles on either side, for a total of two different templates, but three fabric pieces (2–13). To use the soft-edge technique, one larger triangle containing all three pieces would be created, and a background piece would be cut from that triangle. The same triangle template would be used to cut the soft-edge fabric, *cutting to the template* in the places where it would be pieced and *to the fabric* where it would be appliquéd. Illustration 2–14 shows the fabric. A white line indicates the motif that was cut, and a black line indicates the entire template. Illustration 2–15 shows the whole section and 2–16 the completed block.

The second shape, which has been altered with the soft-edge technique, is the large background area behind the remaining points of the

2–13

2–14

2–15

2–12. Spring House

2–16

2–17

2–18

star. To balance out the design, it seemed that a soft design would work there as well. Illustration 2–17 shows the section that was added and 2–18 the completed block.

The idea of soft-edge piecing was so exciting that the group of women who work with me in planning my annual Quilting Seminar and I decided it would be a great theme for the seminar program. We spent a year developing the idea, and many of them made quilts using various aspects of the technique.

Darlene Christopherson decided to try the soft-edge technique on a *Mariner's Compass* design. She made a traditional compass block shown

P2–3. Traditional-style Mariner's Compass block, made by Darlene Christopherson, was the preliminary design for her soft-edge quilt.

P2–4. Detail of Farewell to Mariner's Inn, made by Darlene Christopherson, is a soft-edge version of the traditional Mariner's Compass block.

in photograph P2–3. In that block, each of the 16 outer points has a small wedge "background" piece on either side, forming a still larger wedge. For her soft-edge version, instead of cutting one point and two side pieces, Darlene cut one larger background wedge and then appliquéd a soft-edge "point" to that. She cut away the extra thickness behind the "point" to make it easier to piece into the block. Compare the hard-line original block (P2–3) to the soft-edge block (P2–4) in the center of the quilt. She carried the theme of the patchwork and appliqué throughout her beautiful quilt, *Farewell to Mariner's Inn*.

P2–5. Farewell to Mariner's Inn, *made by Darlene Christopherson, incorporates piecing, appliqué, and the soft-edge technique.*

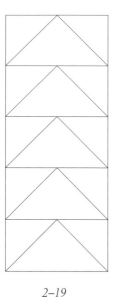

2–19

2–20

2–21

Jay Moody was working on an appliqué project containing birds and flowers. She thought a *Flying Geese* border would be appropriate, but felt the hard line of the patchwork would not be compatible with the softness in her quilt. She decided to use a "soft-edge" *Flying Geese* border. The normal *Flying Geese* pattern contains one large triangle and two smaller ones. Instead of the traditional method, Jay made one larger rectangle template and sketched the larger triangle onto it. She cut a background piece of the entire rectangle and then placed the rectangle template over the various fabrics she wanted to use, still trying to get the

P2–6. Garden Window, *designed, pieced, and appliquéd by Jay Moody and hand-quilted by Gayle Ropp, combines traditional-style appliqué with a soft-edge adaptation of a* Flying Geese *border.*

illusion of the *Flying Geese* triangle, but letting the design of the fabric dictate where the boundaries of the "triangle" would be. Illustration 2–19 shows a line drawing of the basic *Flying Geese* pattern, 2–20 and 2–21 show an example of the type of fabric and motif that could be used for this design. Jay's quilt, *Garden Window*, is shown in photograph P2–6.

Lenore Parham also decided to use the *Flying Geese* pattern for a quilt she made for a new grandchild. In her quilt, she integrated both hard and soft-edge "triangles" for the geese. Her quilt, *Fun Too*, is shown below.

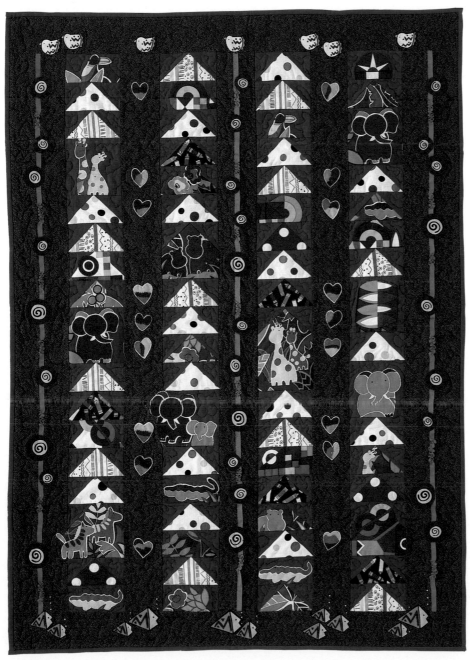

P2–7. Fun Too, made by Lenore Parham, is a hard and soft-edge combination of the traditional Flying Geese *design.*

Yoko Sawanobori found the border print shown below and thought "basket handles." She made her quilt from a traditional-style basket pattern, but used the soft-edge technique for the handles of the basket. She cut the semicircle from the fabric and appliquéd it to the triangle at the top of the baskets. She calls her quilt *Welcome Basket* because of the pineapple on the handles.

2–22

P2–8. Welcome Basket, *made by Yoko Sawanobori, combines a traditional-style basket pattern with soft-edge handles.*

Jay Moody decided to try the soft-edge technique with the *Bow Tie* pattern. The traditional design is shown right (2–23). There are only two templates needed for the pattern, a square and a five-sided shape. Normally the square and two of the five-sided shapes would be dark for the "tie," and the other two pieces would be light for the background. Jay

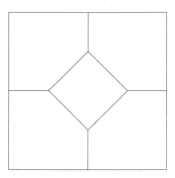

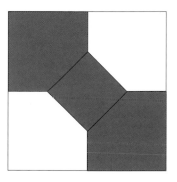

2–23
Bow Tie

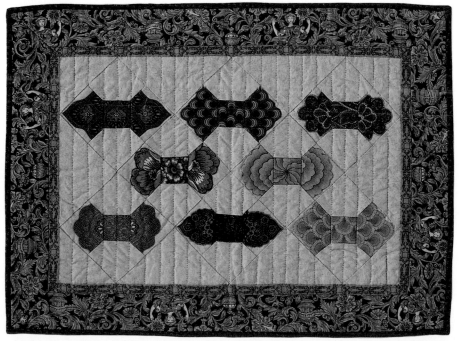

P2–9. Dressed for Success 1, *(top), made by Jay Moody is a traditional-style* Bow Tie *quilt.*
P2–10. Dressed for Success 2, *(bottom), made by Jay Moody, is a soft-edge version of the traditional* Bow Tie *pattern.*

cut all four of the five-sided shapes from the background fabric, but then, using the same template, found places on her fabric to create soft edges on her bow ties. Both the traditional and soft-edge versions of her quilts, *Dressed for Success 1* and *2* are shown on the previous page.

Cindy Blackberg had fun experimenting with border prints, and the soft-edge technique in her quilt shown below. The quilt began with the *Test Tube* design from *Patchwork Portfolio*, but she made alterations to the design. No two blocks are the same since each was cut from a different place on the border print, and a different teal or cranberry print was used in each block. The same teal "onion" fabric was used for the soft-edge technique throughout, thus the name of the quilt, *Testing the Onions*.

P2–11. Testing the Onions, *made by Cindy Blackberg, is a soft-edge adaptation of the pattern* Test Tube.

Chapter 3

THE BASICS OF SOFT-EDGE PIECING

Now that you have had some experience working with border print fabrics in various shapes and designs, and have had an introduction to the soft-edge technique, it is time to take the next step—to experiment and see for yourself how to work with border prints as well as other fabrics to go beyond the confines of the shape and create a soft edge. The main consideration to remember is that this technique combines both piecing and appliqué. Some parts of the shape will be cut following the original template and will be pieced into the design in the normal fashion, while other parts will be appliquéd to a background first, and then the two fabrics will be pieced into the design as if they were one.

THE FABRICS

As you begin experimenting with soft-edge piecing, you will find yourself looking at fabrics in a completely different light. The main consideration is to look for fabrics that have edges that will lend themselves to appliqué—edges that can be cut out creating an interesting motif. Chapter 1 explains how I like to have lines on border prints outline or frame the various shapes. Likewise with soft-edge piecing, I look for prints with motifs that have lines, which will frame the soft piece. I cut $1/8''$ out from the line and turn under that portion, leaving the line showing to "outline" the soft edge.

However, it is not essential that a fabric have a line such as this in order to be used to create a soft edge. Fabrics with gradual curves or motifs that have edges, which would be easy to turn under and appliqué, are also suitable to use. Many border prints have excellent motifs for creating soft edges. Florals and paisleys also are good prints to look for. A few examples of prints that work well for soft edges, along with motifs cut from them are shown in Illustration 3–1.

3–1

Some fabrics with a single motif repeated over and over, such as the shell fabric in Illustration 3–2, may seem limiting in terms of soft-edge possibilities, but if the design is a mirror-image pattern, there are countless ways in which that type of fabric can be used. *Facets,* shown below, illustrates some of the possibilities. The traditional style block is shown in Illustration 3–3, but if I wanted to change the wide points to a soft edge, and planned on using the shell fabric, a single motif cut from that fabric (3–4) might look nice in the points, but would not fill the space as much as I would like (3–5).

3–2

3–3. *Facets*

3–4

3–5

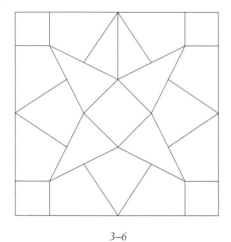

3–6

To fill more of the space, two mirror-imaged pieces can be cut, seamed down the middle, and then appliquéd as one piece. The drawing of *Facets* has a line indicating half of the original point (3–6), which is the piece that was used as the template for the mirror image. Illustration 3–7 shows the template placed on the fabric and mirror-imaged with a white line indicating the finished piece. Illustrations 3–8 and 3–9 show the two pieces separated and then put together. Finally compare the finished block (3–10) with the first soft-edge variation (3–5) to see how different the fabric motif can look cut as a single motif or with two pieces mirror-imaged. Two additional variations of mirror-imaged motifs cut from the same "shell" fabric are shown in Illustrations 3–11 and 3–12.

3–7

3–8 3–9

3–10

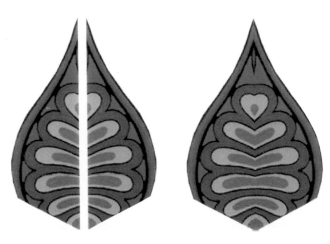

3–11

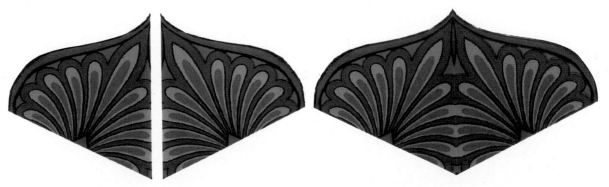

3–12

Many distinct mirror-imaged variations can be created from a single motif, ranging from a wide angle to a narrow one. One way to discover what mirror images will look like is to place a single mirror on a symmetrical motif in the fabric and move it around to see all the possibilities. Illustration 3–13 shows two more fabrics, with mirror images cut from them.

3–13

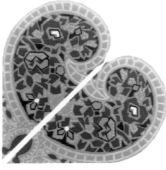

Fabrics that have symmetrical motifs are particularly useful, but don't completely pass over ones, which do not have mirror images. Asymmetrical motifs can also be quite effective for designing a block with soft-edge piecing. See the soft-edged *Dressed For Success* quilt made by Jay Moody on page 45 for an example of non-mirror-imaged motifs and how effective they can be when used with the soft-edge technique.

If there is a fabric you particularly like, but which has edges that would be difficult to turn under neatly, smooth out the uneven edges by cutting out from the motif just a little. The smoother edge will then be easier to appliqué. Or appliqué without turning the edges under at all, and sew the edges down with a fine buttonhole stitch. This technique is used in *broderie perse* and is explained in Chapter 5, page 103.

Later chapters will deal more fully with construction, technique, and design. For now, to help you understand more of the basics, it is best to go back to the individual shapes on page 18 and see how portions of those geometric shapes can be changed from hard to soft lines.

There are two basic ways to consider the soft edge on individual shapes. One way has the soft edge extending *beyond* the boundaries of the original shape, and the other has the soft edge contained *within* the boundaries of the individual shape. For example, the illustrations here and on the next page show the square, octagon, triangle, and diamond with soft edges both within the original shapes and extending beyond the original shape. Study these examples and then do the following exercise to gain experience in understanding how the soft-edge technique works.

SHAPE

SOFT EDGE EXTENDED

SOFT EDGE CONTAINED

3–14

SHAPE

SOFT EDGE EXTENDED

SOFT EDGE CONTAINED

3–15

3–16

3–17

3–18 ▶

CREATING SOFT EDGES IN INDIVIDUAL SHAPES

For this series of exercises, you will need all of the supplies listed on page 18. The only exception is that the "fabric" photocopy must be one in which there are possibilities for cutting motifs with soft edges. The border prints shown on pages 19 and 20 are suitable to use as well as the fabrics shown here. For a matter of comparison, if you used one of these borders for the previous exercises, you may want to use the same one for this exercise. That way you can see the difference and compare the hard-edge version to the soft-edge one.

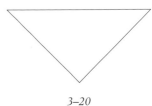

3–20

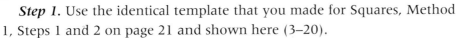

EXERCISE 6

Soft Edge Extending Beyond Original Square

METHOD 1

The square in this method is broken up by dividing it diagonally from corner to corner to create four triangles, exactly as was done with Squares, Method 1 in Exercise 1 on page 21. The four triangles will be sewn together along the same seam lines (in this case since you are working in paper, they will be glued) just as that square was done. The difference between this square and that one is that portions of the fabric will extend beyond the outer perimeter of the square. Since the seams will be pieced as far as the *corners* of the original square, any portion that extends beyond the original square must be appliquéd onto a background.

Step 1. Use the identical template that you made for Squares, Method 1, Steps 1 and 2 on page 21 and shown here (3–20).

Step 2. Place the triangle template over the fabric and move it around until the outer corners of the triangle (points A) fall on an area of the design that can be appliquéd outward from those points. In other words, you need an appliquéable edge to carry on from where the seam leaves off. See Illustrations 3–21 and 3–22 for examples of what does and does not work.

Step 3. If you are curious to see what the design will look like, place the mirrors along the two short edges of the triangle, at the same angle as the template. If you are satisfied with what you see in the mirror, mark along the template on the two short sides (the edges that will be pieced). Cut along the marked lines, then outward from the two corners, following the design on the fabric. When you are actually doing this in fabric, you will add the seam allowance along the pieced edges

3–21
The appliqué motif extends from the edges of the template and therefore will work.

3–22
The appliqué motif comes from the center of the template and therefore will not work.

◀ *3–19*

and cut enough extra to have an edge to turn under for appliquéing along the soft edges. Illustration 3–23 shows the motif that was cut from the fabric in Illustration 3–21.

Step 4. Mark some part of the design on the template as a reference point, and cut three more "triangles" identical to the first. Glue the four of them together on a piece of paper (3–24). If this method was being done in fabric, the finished "square" would be appliquéd *onto* the block.

3–23

METHOD 2

The square in this method is broken up by dividing it into four smaller squares as was done in Squares, Method 2, on page 22. Follow Steps 1 and 2 for that method. Sides AD and DC will be pieced and sides AB and BC will have the soft edge (3–25).

3–24

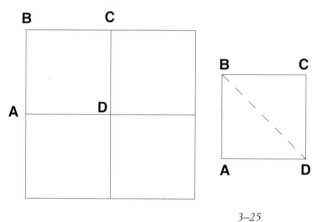

3–25

Step 3. Place the template *diagonally* on the photocopied fabric, and move it around until you find an appliquéable motif, which could begin at points A and C (3–26). Mark along lines AD and DC, then remove the template. Cut along the marked lines, then cut the remaining part out following the motif in the fabric (3–27). (Once again, because you are working on paper, do not add seam or turn-under allowances. When you begin actual sewing, then special attention must be paid to allowing for seams.)

Step 4. Mark part of the design on the template as a guide. Then, using that reference point, cut three more identical "squares" and glue them together on a piece of paper (3–28).

3–26

3–27

3–28

Squares With the Soft Edge Contained Within the Shape

There are several different ways in which you can add the soft edge within the shape. The two most common are to bring the soft edge in from the outside of the square or to take it out from the middle. I prefer bringing it in from the sides since I like to have a "frame" from the border around the edges. You can choose to do it either way for this exercise. In either case the entire shape would have to be cut from a background fabric and the soft-edge fabric is placed upon that background. For this exercise, your background will be paper but the illustrations here show it in fabric.

3–29

METHOD 1: COMING FROM THE CENTER OUTWARD

Make the square either from the triangle template or small square template exactly as was done in the previous two examples. The difference this time is that the motif will fit within the triangle or square. That completed motif will then be appliquéd onto the background square (3–29).

METHOD 2: COMING FROM THE EDGE INWARD

Step 1. Use the same triangle template shown in Illustration 3–20. If you were doing this in fabric, you would cut one large square from the background print. Since you are doing it on paper, trace the square that the triangle template came from onto a piece of paper, and divide it diagonally from corner to corner. This will give you a base upon which to paste your pieces.

Step 2. Place the triangle template on the fabric, and move it around until you find a soft edge that will fall completely *within* the triangle. I

3–30

like using a border print for this method so that I can still place a line from the fabric on the long edge of the triangle to "frame" the square. Mark along the triangle template in the places that will be *pieced,* and cut along the fabric design in the places that will be *appliquéd,* as shown in Illustration 3–30.

Step 3. Mark some part of the design from the fabric onto the template so that you will have a guide for cutting the remaining three "triangles." Cut three more pieces identical to the first (3–31a).

Step 4. Paste the soft-edge pieces onto the square (3–31b). If you were actually sewing these, you would first sew the corners of each soft piece together forming a square with a hole in the middle, then baste it down, appliqué it to the background, and finally cut away the excess fabric from behind the appliqué pieces before sewing it into another part of the block. The soft-edge square in Illustration 3–14 on page 53 was cut from the same border and only shifted ¼" from the location of the one in Illustration 3–31b, yet they look quite different.

3–31a

3–31b

3–32

Soft-Edge Octagon

The soft-edge octagon is made the same as the hard-edge one, except that, just as in the examples of the square, the triangle template is centered so that a portion of the design on the fabric will extend from the edges of the seams, as shown in Illustration 3–32. Cut eight identical "triangles," and paste them onto a piece of paper. The illustrations here show the fabric (3–32), the single motif cut out (3–33), and eight of them put together (3–34).

Illustration 3–35 shows another octagon cut from the same fabric. The two seem very dissimilar to each other, but the only difference is that the template for Illustration 3–35 was simply flipped upside down from the way it was placed on the fabric in Illustration 3–32. Select a fabric to work with, and see how many different soft-edge octagons you can make from the same fabric.

3–33

3–34

3–35

EXERCISE 9

Soft-Edge Triangles

The soft-edge technique can be used on the triangle in one of two ways. In both cases the shorter side of the triangle is the one that is pieced into the design and the longer edges are the ones that contain the soft edge.

METHOD 1

If you want to maintain the *illusion* of a triangle in the finished design, this method requires finding a fabric that has a motif shaped very similar to the triangle. The possibilities are more limited as only a single piece is cut out. With the next method, there will be more versatility because *two* pieces will be cut; thus there is more chance to manipulate the images.

Use the triangle template from Octagons, Step 1 on page 24, and draw a line down the middle of it to use for centering. Place the template on the fabric, and move it around until a part of the motif extends from the corners at the base of the triangle. Remember that the appliquéd edge must start where the piecing ends so the placement of the template is very important. The straight line at the base of the triangle is the part where the seam will be, and the other edges will be appliquéd as shown in the illustrations below.

3–36

3–37

METHOD 2

This method requires dividing the triangle in half lengthwise and then mirror-imaging the two halves.

Step 1. Divide the triangle the same as Triangles, Hard Edge, Steps 1 and 2 on page 25, making sure that the arrow on the template is along the *long* side of the triangle. This long edge is the part that will be appliquéd, and the two shorter sides will be pieced (3–38).

Step 2. Place the template on the fabric, and move it around so that an appliquéable edge will begin and end from points A and B. Now is a good time to check to make sure you like what the design will be, so place a single mirror along side BC. Carefully remove the template and look into the mirror to see what the mirror-imaged motif will look like.

Step 3. If you are satisfied with the image, mark part of the design from the fabric directly onto the template. This time, you will want to mark quite a bit of the design because mirror-imaging can be more confusing when working with soft edges than when working with border prints. The difference is that with soft edge, the template might be placed in almost any direction on the fabric in order to have the appliquéable edge in the right place, whereas with border prints, it is usually placed on the straight or cross grain of the fabric, making it easier to see the mirrored image.

Step 4. Mark the fabric along the two short edges of the template, cut along those two edges, and then cut following the *design* of the fabric on the other edge (3–39).

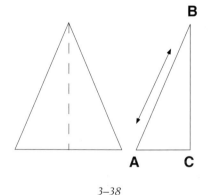

3–38

Step 5. Carefully flip the template and cut another mirror-imaged piece identical to the first as illustrated below (3–39 to 3–41).

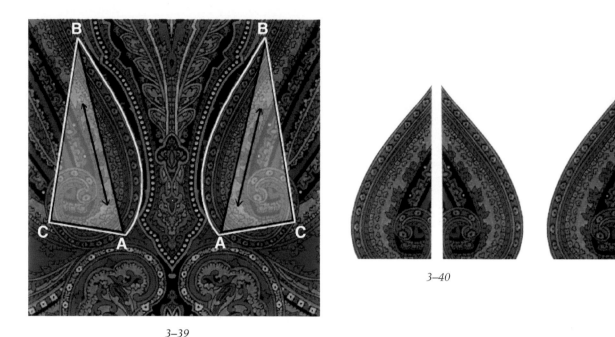

3–39

3–40

3–41

EXERCISE 10

Soft-Edge Diamonds

There are many different ways to add a soft edge to a diamond. Try the three methods here, and then have fun discovering other ways on your own.

METHOD 1

The majority of diamonds in patchwork designs are parts of stars, with the diamonds coming together at the center of a block. When working with a diamond in this type of design, I usually like to leave the *inside* portions of the diamonds to be pieced and create a soft edge on the outer portions. Therefore, I would tend to divide the diamond sideways, and then stop the lengthwise mark when it met the other line as in Illustration 3–42. If the diamond *was* part of a star, I might make either a hard-line octagon in the center from a border or a soft-edged octagon. The soft-edge technique would then be used on the two smaller triangles, which would be made in identically the same way as the triangle was made in the previous exercise. To make the diamond, do the following steps.

Step 1. Divide the diamond from page 18 according to the diagram in

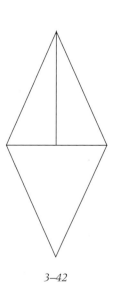

3–42

3–43

3–44

3–45

3–46

Illustration 3–42, and make both larger and smaller triangle templates. (If you did the previous example, you can use those same templates.)

Step 2. Create a soft-edge "triangle" cut from the two small triangles as you did in the previous sections as shown in the right-hand portion of Illustration 3–43. This will be the outer part of the diamond.

Step 3. For the bottom part of the diamond cut a hard-line triangle from a border print as shown in the left-hand portion of Illustration 3–43, and paste it along with the soft-edge triangle onto a piece of paper (3–44 and 3–45).

Step 4. Put your two mirrors along the bottom of the triangle, and look into them to see what eight of the diamonds put together would look like (3–46).

METHOD 2, VARIATION 1

This next variation has the soft edge contained entirely *within* the diamond. When working with a diamond, which forms a star, I would rarely use this method as that usually entails mirror-imaging four different pieces, and would therefore result in *16* points coming together at the center of the star. Eight are difficult enough, but 16 are almost impossible to piece accurately. There are times, however, when the diamonds do not form part of a star, where this technique might be useful or where you could find a motif in the fabric that does not require that two pieces be mirror-imaged on each point of the diamond. I like using a border print for this method so that I can "frame" the outside of the diamond with a small line.

Step 1. Divide the diamond on page 18 in half both lengthwise and crosswise to create four smaller triangles. Put an arrow along the *long* edges of the four triangles and mark two opposite triangles with an O and the other two with an X. The pieces marked with an O will be cut identically and those marked with an X will be the mirror image of the O's as shown in Illustration 3–47.

Step 2. Make a template from the entire diamond as well as from the smaller triangle. If you were doing this in fabric, you would cut a "background" piece using the diamond template and adding seam allowances. As you are working in paper, trace around the diamond onto a piece of paper so that you will have a guide for pasting the pieces.

Step 3. Place the small triangle template onto the border print fabric with the arrow along a line in the border (3–48). Move it around until you find a suitable "soft edge" to use. Cut two pieces identical to this, and then *flip* the template horizontally and find the identical, but mirror-imaged repeat of the design for the other two pieces (3–49).

Step 4. Cut the pieces out, and glue them to the piece of paper with the traced diamond (3–50).

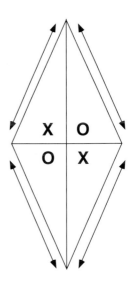

3–47

3–48

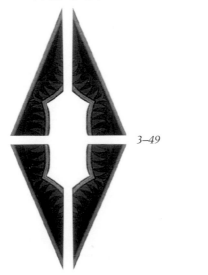

3–49

3–50

METHOD 2, VARIATION 2

Step 1. For this variation cut the diamond in half sideways (3–51) and make a template from the triangle.

Step 2. Draw the diamond on a piece of paper. (In fabric a background piece would be cut.)

Step 3. Find an entire motif from the fabric that fits within the triangle (3–52 to 3–53).

Step 4. Cut another identical piece and glue both pieces to the paper diamond (3–54).

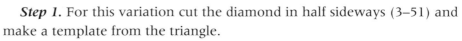

3–51

3–52

3–53

3–54

METHOD 2, VARIATION 3

Variation 3 also divides the diamond in half sideways, but in this case the soft edge will be only on *two* sides and will fall *outside* the template. The arrow in Illustration 3–55 indicates where the soft edge will be. The template is the same triangle used in the last variation. The soft edge will fall along line AB; the two triangles will be mirror-imaged and pieced together along line BC.

Step 1. Mark the template with an arrow, and place it on the fabric until you can find an area where the soft edge will come completely from the side marked with the arrow. Draw part of the design onto the template.

Step 2. Cut along the edge of the template on the sides to be pieced and along the fabric design on the parts to be appliquéd. Carefully flip the template and find the identical mirror-imaged motif. Cut the second piece out and glue both to a piece of paper (3–56 to 3–58).

I urge you to either photocopy the pages from this book or copy your own fabric, and create both the hard-edge and soft-edge versions of each of these shapes. You will gain a much greater understanding of the concept if you actually do the exercises yourself, as opposed to merely reading about them in the book. If you have fabrics that you want to eventually use, it would be best for you to work with photocopies of your own fabrics. It is fun seeing all of the possibilities that can come from cutting the fabrics in so many different ways.

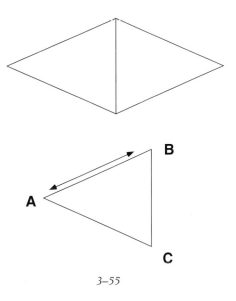

3–55

3–56

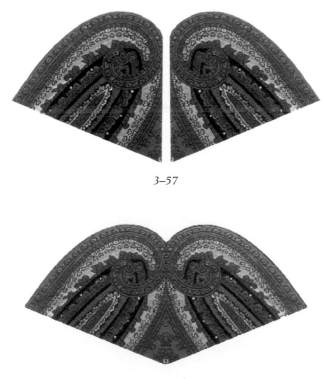

3–57

3–58

Chapter 4

THE SOFT-EDGE TECHNIQUE IN A TRADITIONAL GEOMETRIC DESIGN

Having had the practice of creating soft edges on various shapes, it is time to look at traditional-style quilt designs and see where changes could be made to create soft edges within the block. First and foremost, my experience has been that, in general, the more simple blocks lend themselves better to this technique. The soft edge, in itself, creates such interest that it is not necessary to have a complex pattern to generate the impact of the design.

There are numerous ways to apply soft edges to a design, and every time I teach, someone in the class comes up with yet another variation. The purpose here is to give you several ideas, but I would hope that you will continue to experiment. Furthermore, every fabric you choose will give a completely different effect and will suggest other possibilities.

The simple *Eight-Pointed Star* (4–1 and 4–2) has been selected to illustrate some of the soft-edge possibilities. The same soft-edge fabric has been used in the following illustrations to show you that many different effects can be created from one single fabric. Study each of the examples and then do exercises 11–13 using either photocopies of your own fabric or copies of one of the pages in this book.

1. One possibility is to leave the basic star alone and add a soft edge that appears to be coming from *behind* the points of the star. In these examples (4–3 to 4–4), the soft edge would be appliquéd to the outer

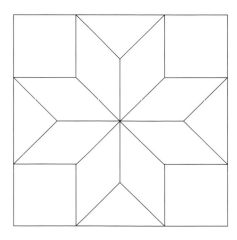

4–1
Eight-Pointed Star

4–2

squares and triangles and then those would be pieced into the star. Refer to the photograph of my quilt *Olde World Star* on page 109 to see where a soft edge appears to be coming from behind the star points on both the inner and outer stars of the block.

2. You might try adding a soft edge to the *corners* of the star (4–5 to 4–6).

3. The soft edge can also be contained entirely *within* the star points (4–7 to 4–9).

But don't be limited by only bringing the soft edge from the center of the star. It can also come from the outer tip of the point. For example, see what happens when the *same* pieces of fabric used in Illustrations 4–7 to 4–9 are turned around. The hard edges of the shapes are now on the outside along the edges forming the star points, and the soft edges are pointing *inward* toward the center of the star. It is amazing what

4–3

4–4

4–5

4–6

4–7

4–8

4–9

4–10

4–11

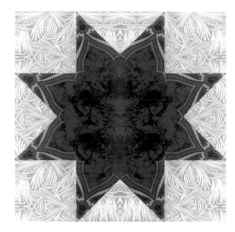

4–12

4–13

totally different effects are achieved simply by reversing the direction of the pieces (4–10 to 4–12).

4. Yet another variation would be to contain the soft edge within the points, but to do it on *both* sides of the diamond, instead of one side. Illustrations 4–13 and 4–14 use the identical diamond, but the diamonds have been reversed, giving a totally different effect in each star. The star in Illustration 4–15 uses the identical soft-edge piece on both sides of the diamond. In fact it is the same piece that was used on one side of the diamond in Illustration 4–12 above.

5. A soft-edge "border" can be added around the points of the star (4–16). In this case, the star would be cut from the fabric in the normal manner, and the soft edge would actually be appliquéd to the pieces surrounding the star. This technique was used by Janine Holzman in her quilt (P4–1).

4–14

4–15

4–16

P4–1. Magic, *made by Janine Holzman, is a soft-edge variation of the traditional-style* Lone Star *design*

6. More than one of these techniques can be applied at the same time. In each of the cases below, only soft-edge motifs from the previous examples have been used, but the additional soft-edge motifs in the block dramatically change the appearance.

4–17

4–18

4–19

4–20

4–21

4–22

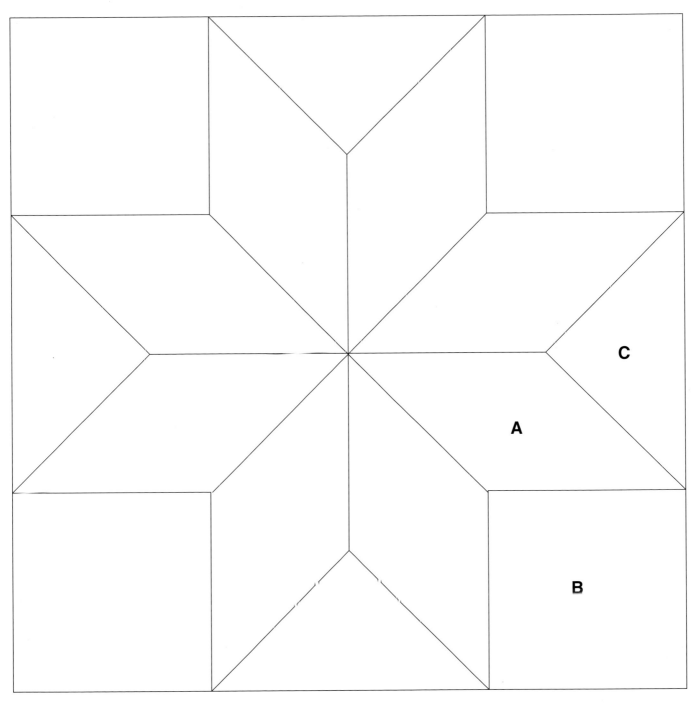

4–23
Eight-Pointed Star

Eight-Pointed Star

Studying the illustrations of the soft-edge *Eight-Pointed Star* on the previous pages should give you many ideas for working with different fabrics in simple designs, but you will learn even more if you try the technique yourself and do the following exercise.

The supplies needed for this exercise are:

At least four line drawings of an *Eight-Pointed Star* approximately 7". Draw your own or photocopy the one on page 73.

Photocopies at 64% reduction of a border print or other fabric, which has soft-edge possibilities. Either photocopy one of the fabric illustrations on pages 19–20 or 55–56 or one of your own fabrics.

- Transparent template material
- Permanent red marker
- Paper-cutting scissors
- Glue stick
- Tracing paper

You will learn more if you try each of the six methods described on pages 68–72. This exercise will go step-by-step through the first two, and after doing those, you should be able to do the rest yourself by studying the illustrations and referring to Chapter 3 on how to make soft edges on individual shapes. Before doing any of these methods, you should do the following:

Step 1. Make templates from the *Eight-Pointed Star* for the diamond (A), triangle (C), and square (B). Since at this point you are working on paper, do not add a seam allowance to the templates.

Step 2. Using a right-angle (90°) triangle as explained on page 21, draw a line down the middle of the triangle template. Divide the diamond and square in half by connecting point-to-point as in Illustration 4–25. These lines will be your guide for centering the templates on the fabric (4–25).

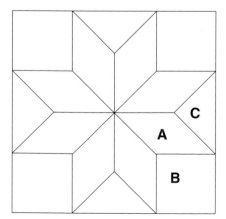

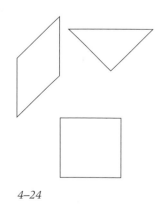

4–24

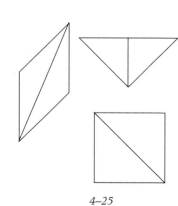

4–25

4–26

4–27

METHOD 1: POINTS THAT APPEAR TO BE COMING FROM BEHIND THE STAR

Step 1. Begin by creating a soft edge that appears to be coming from behind the points of the star. If you want the same motif in all eight places, use the triangle template for the soft edge, or draw a line across the square to indicate where the triangle will be. If the square is used with no line on it, there is the risk of cutting a piece too large for the triangles along the sides of the block. Place the triangle (or square divided into triangles) template on the photocopy of the fabric, and center it on some motif in the fabric that you would like to use for the soft edge.

Step 2. Draw a portion of the design you have chosen directly onto the template with the red marker (4–26).

Step 3. Mark along the edges of the triangle where the shape will be *pieced*, and cut along those edges, but then follow the *fabric* design to cut the part that will be appliquéd (4–27).

Step 6. Cut seven more motifs identical to the first and paste them onto one of the copies of the *Eight-Pointed Star*. Refer to Illustration 4–3 on page 69 to see what this particular shape looks like when added to the *Eight-Pointed Star*.

➡ NOTE: *If you do not like the size or angle of the piece that is to be cut from the fabric, you can always try mirror-imaging portions of the design to create a completely different-sized shape as was described on pages 33, 50–52, 63–64, and 67.*

METHOD 2: ADDING A SOFT EDGE TO THE CORNERS OF THE SQUARE

This method can be done by cutting a single piece and applying it to the corners as was done in Illustrations 4–5 and 4–22 or by cutting two mirror-imaged pieces and actually having them "frame" the sides of the square. Adding a *single* piece to the corners is basically no different than adding a piece appearing to come from behind the points of the star as was done on the previous pages. In both cases, you will be working with a right angle from either the square or triangle templates. Therefore, this explanation will only pertain to working with two mirror-imaged pieces in the corners of the block.

Step 1. As you will be working with two pieces, you will need to divide the corner square in half diagonally from the corner inward as shown in Illustration 4–28. The template you will use is one half of that square. In fact you do not actually need to make a new template because half of the square is the *same* as the triangle at the sides of the block. If you made that triangle template earlier, you already have the piece you need. If you look at the illustration of the *Eight-Pointed Star* in Illustration 4–28, you will see that half of the corner square (1) is the same as the triangle in the center of the sides of the block (2).

Step 2. Place the template on the fabric photocopy so that the soft edge will be coming from side AC. Find an area that you think might look good, and if you are unsure, place your mirror along side AB of the template to see what the mirror-imaged effect will be (4–29).

Step 3. When you are satisfied, draw and then cut along line AC and portions of BC and AB if necessary for the design you have chosen. Then cut along the fabric design for the rest of the piece.

Step 4. Carefully mark part of the design from the fabric onto the template. Then *flip* the template over, and find an identical mirror-

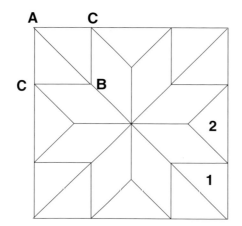

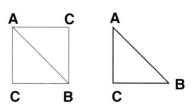

4–28

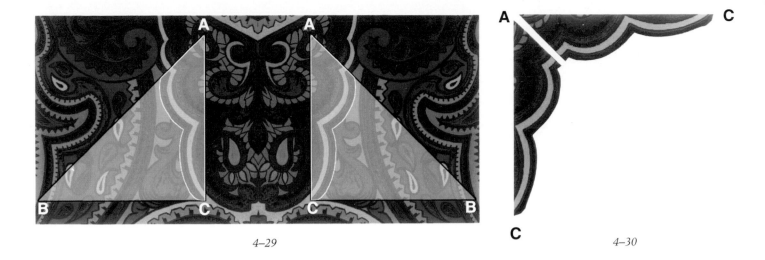

4–29

4–30

imaged place on another part of the fabric (4–29). Cut this piece out the same as the previous one, and glue the two pieces to the corner of the square (4–30).

Step 5. Repeat for the other three corners.

Refer to Illustrations 4–6, 4–16, 4–19, and 4–20 for examples of what these two mirror-imaged motifs look like in the star. Note that 4–16 and 4–20 have simply reversed the placement of the pieces so that they are against the star points instead of in the corner.

With all of the soft-edge variations that can be added to a design as simple as the *Eight-Pointed Star*, it is exciting to then look at other traditional designs and see how many possibilities there are.

On pages 15–16, you saw how different a single design, *Rolling Star,* can look depending on how the border print is used. Next look at that same design once more and see how the soft-edge technique completely changes it yet again. The blocks shown on the next page correspond to the examples shown earlier. For example compare Illustration 4–31 to 1–21 on page 16. The only difference in Illustration 4–31 is that a *soft edge* appearing to be coming from behind the star points has been added. A soft edge has been added between the points of the star and the corners on Illustration 4–32, which is the same as 1–18 on page 15 except for those two changes. Illustration 4–33 corresponds to 1–20 on page 16 except for the soft-edge octagon in the center of the block and the soft motif added to the diamonds along the outer portions of the design.

4–31

4–32

4–33

Where To Add a Soft Edge

The following exercise will help you to learn how to look at traditional-style patchwork designs and change some of the hard lines in those designs to soft ones. The more actual experimenting you do, the more you will learn. You will need:

- Pencil
- Tracing paper
- A book of many traditional designs or use the designs shown on the facing page (4–34).

The designs in Illustration 4–34 contain some of the blocks, which I have created over the last four years. These particular ones were selected as I thought they offered good soft-edge possibilities.

Step 1. Place a piece of tracing paper over the designs, and sketch curved motifs in the places where you think a soft edge would look good.

Step 2. After you have finished each design, take a new piece of tracing paper and try to find completely different places to add the soft edge technique.

Working through this exercise will cause you to look at traditional-style designs in a totally different way and will give you ideas for adding the soft edge to a block with fabric photocopies in the next exercise.

Adding the Soft Edge to Traditional-Style Designs

Use one of the 7" blocks on pages 80–81 (*Ferris Wheel* or *Turnabout*) or on pages 29–30 (*Atlantic Jewel* or *La Mancha*) and photocopies of the fabrics in this book. Alternatively, draw your own design and copy your own fabric. If you have a fabric that offers good soft-edge possibilities, it would be best to use your own. The designs on the following pages are 7" in size, which is approximately 64% of an 11" block. The fabrics illustrated have also been reduced by 64%. If you want to use your own fabrics in place of the ones here, you should also reduce your fabric by 64% when it is photocopied in order to see what it would look like in an 11" block.

Following all the steps you did previously to add soft edges to shapes and the *Eight-Pointed Star*, select the areas on your design where you would like to try the soft-edge technique and have fun playing with all of the possibilities.

Chateau

Bachelor Bouquet

Facets

Irish Star

Chelsea

Sunset Star

Prairie Points

Charlotte's Web

Mystery Rose

Bellflower

Memory Star

Centennial Star

Deco Tulip

Ferris Wheel

Turnabout

Seaflower

Signal Light 91

Northern Lights 94

Springtime Star

La Mancha

4–35
Ferris Wheel

4–36
Turnabout

Chapter 5

CONSTRUCTION TECHNIQUES

By now you should be ready to forget the photocopies and go to fabric! This chapter will cover all the topics you need to start your project, from drafting the pattern and making templates to actual sewing.

There are two basic ways in which the soft edge can be added to a patchwork design. In the first, it is pieced and then appliquéd *onto* the block, and in the second it is appliquéd to a background and then pieced *into* the block. (The part being appliquéd might also consist of more than one piece, which would be sewn together prior to the appliqué, but once the appliqué is complete, that section would still be pieced into the block.) It will be necessary for you to either draft your own design in the size needed, or to work with a pattern that shows the design in full size. Usually two or more shapes will be combined to create a larger background piece onto which the soft edge will be appliquéd. Therefore any time you want to change the design to accommodate a soft edge, you will have to go back to the original drafted block to make the alterations needed for the new templates.

As an example, look at the design, *Sunset Star*, shown below. Let's suppose that you have decided to make the center octagon in the soft-edge technique and that you also want to do the soft-edge technique to the eight small squares.

5–1. Sunset Star

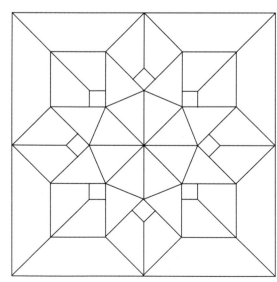

To change the small squares in the design to soft edges, a new "background" template will have to be created. In the original design, there are two "background" pieces on either side of the small squares. For a soft edge, one larger square template, which encompasses the area of all three pieces, is needed. For a guide, lightly mark the outline of the small square onto the template. A background piece will be cut from the entire large square template. Then that same template will be placed over the soft-edge fabric and moved around until a motif is found that gives the illusion of the small square (5–2). That portion of the fabric will be cut along the motif, and the remaining will be cut following the template.

Next, the soft-edge motif will be appliquéd to the background. Cut away from behind the appliqué to eliminate the extra layer of fabric, and then piece that section *into* the design, the same as would be done if the section had been made out of the three original pieces. The illustrations below show the piece of fabric from which the soft-edge "square" was cut and the background fabric upon which it was appliquéd.

5–2

5–3

The soft-edge "octagon" for the center of the block would be made the same way as was explained on page 60. A template would be made from one of the triangles in the center of the block. Eight identical "triangles" would be cut with the soft edge on the smaller side of the triangle. Then they would be pieced together to form an octagon with the soft edges around the outside of the shape as illustrated below.

5–4

5–5

5–6

The edges of the "octagon" would then be turned under and basted down to be ready for appliqué. *But you have to have something on which to appliqué that octagon.* In the original design, the star is formed from eight triangles in the center creating the octagon and eight triangles outside of that forming the points of the star. One center triangle and one point of the star put together would form a diamond. Now you will have to create a diamond template, which is a combination of both those triangles, and piece eight diamonds together to make a star. This will then give a base. After the entire block has been pieced together (5–7), the octagon

5–7

5–8

can then be appliquéd on top of the star (5–8). It would be very difficult to appliqué the octagon only to the triangle points of the star, as there would be a hole in the middle of the block. After the appliqué is complete, the extra fabric from the star can be carefully cut away from behind the octagon to eliminate thickness.

When this block was complete, it seemed that there was too much light background fabric showing, so I made a new block, and this time added a mirror-imaged soft-edge "border" to two of the four sides of the squares (This technique is explained in detail on pages 76–77). Using the same square template, I divided it in half diagonally, then moved the template around on the fabric until it exposed a motif I would like to use. The fabric and templates on the fabric are shown in Illustration 5–9. This border was appliquéd to the background square along with the small soft-edge "square" as is shown in Illustration 5–10. The excess fabric was cut away from behind *both* soft-edge pieces, and that entire square was pieced *into* the block. Compare this new version of the block (5–11) with the previous one (5–8) to see what a difference this small change makes.

5–10

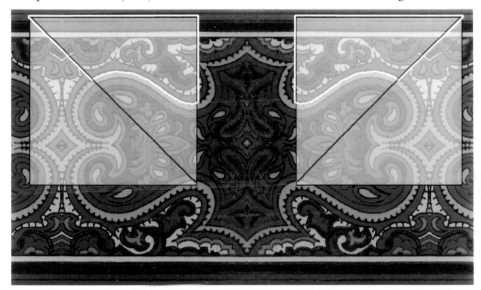

5–9

5–11

DRAFTING THE PATTERN

Patterns for eight of my original quilt block designs are on pages 126–143, as well as patterns for *Rolling Star* and the basic *Eight-Pointed Star*. You can see why it is important to have at least one fourth of the full-sized block of your design to work with and how it would be difficult to create the soft edge if only individual templates were given. For this reason, the patterns in this book show at least one fourth of the entire design, so that there will be enough to go on to make the templates needed for the soft-edge variation you choose. All of the patterns are for an 11″ finished block.

Depending on the design and fabric that are chosen for the soft-edge technique, you may want to make your block in a different size than the one given here. Knowing how to draft your own patterns is, in my opinion, one of the most important aspects of patchwork. Therefore, I feel it is important to give a brief explanation on pattern drafting here. (For a complete explanation on pattern drafting see *Patchwork Patterns* and *Patchwork Portfolio* listed in the bibliography.)

Almost all geometric designs used in patchwork fall into one of several different categories. That category is basically a grid, and the design is drawn by connecting various parts of the grid. The whole secret to knowing how to draft your own patterns is first to be able to recognize which grid category a design falls into, and second how to get that grid onto a piece of paper.

Learning to recognize which category or grid a design falls into is a matter of being able to see how the design is broken up. You do not always clearly see the grid in a design. It is necessary, in your mind, to be able to super-impose that grid over the design. The basic categories are shown here. They include a square being broken into 4, 16, 64, 9, 36, 25, and 49 smaller squares. The 4, 16, and 64 square grids are considered the "four-patch" category. The 9 and 36 square grids are the "nine-patch" category, and the 25 and 49 square grids are the "five-patch" and "seven-patch" categories respectively (5–12).

The *Eight-Pointed Star* falls in yet another category. It is very different from the others in that it is not based on a grid of equal squares, but on a grid of lines radiating from the center outward in equal *angles*.

The easiest way to put the grid of squares onto a piece of paper is to work with a piece of graph paper. Graph paper can be bought in large sheets with various-sized divisions, and if you keep several different tablets on hand, you may be able to use those for most of your drafting needs. Odd-size squares may not fit onto the graph paper, however, so it is good to know how to get the grid onto a blank square of paper. While there are many methods for doing so, there is one very simple technique, which I will explain here.

All you need is a ruler *longer* than the size of the square. Decide how many *equal* divisions are needed across the paper for the particular grid you are creating and, starting with zero, find the same number of equal divisions on the ruler, making sure that they end up *longer* than the width of the paper you are dividing.

In other words, to divide an 11½″ square of paper into four equal divisions for a 16-square grid, you would need to find four equal divisions on the ruler that ended up *longer* than 11½″, which in this case would be 12″ (Illustration 5–13 on page 88).

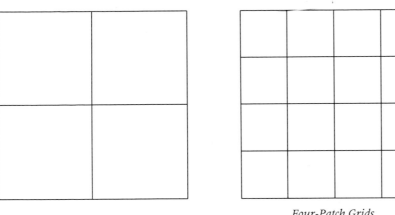 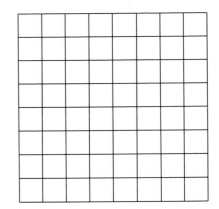

Four-Patch Grids

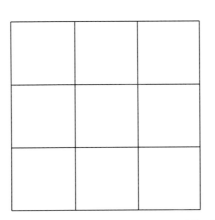 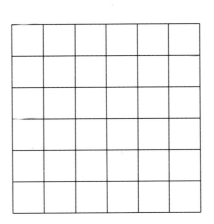

Nine-Patch Grids

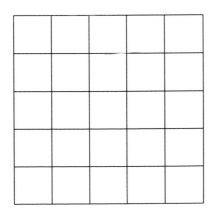 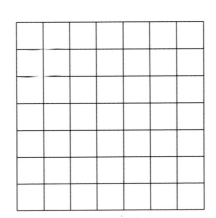 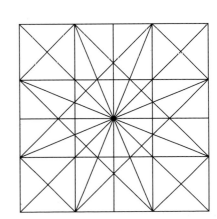

Five-Patch Grid *Seven-Patch Grid* *Eight-Pointed Star Grid*

5–12

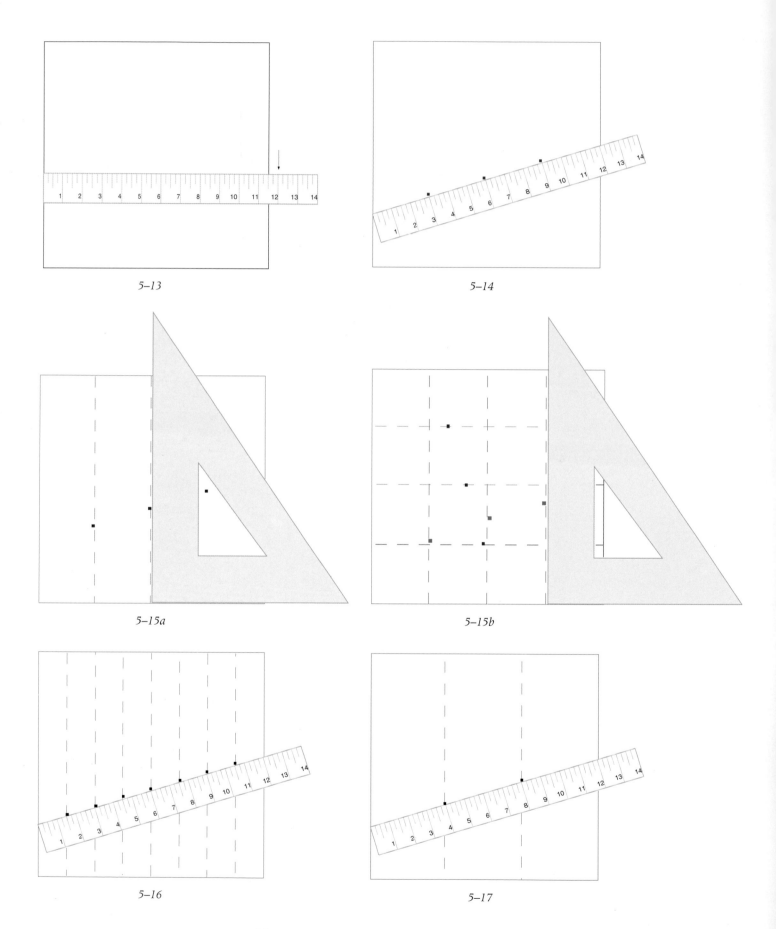

5–13

5–14

5–15a

5–15b

5–16

5–17

It is very easy to divide 12″ into four equal divisions, but not as easy to divide 11½″. All you have to do is *pretend* the paper is 12″ by angling the 12″ on the ruler across the width of the square. Starting with zero on one side, angle the ruler until 12″ hits the parallel and opposite side (5–14). Then all you have to do is make a mark every three inches to get the four equal divisions.

Place a right-angle (90°) triangle along the bottom of the square, line the side of it up to each dot, and draw the lines of the first side of the grid. These lines are indicated in red on Illustration 5–15a. Then turn the paper one quarter turn, make a new set of dots in a different color (so as not to make the mistake of going to the wrong dot) and repeat the procedure (5–15b).

To help you understand the technique more clearly, the same 11½″ square is shown, but with the ruler placed on it in the different positions necessary to divide the square for each of the other categories.

For a 64-square grid, where eight equal divisions are needed, go to 12″ and make a mark every 1½″ (5–16).

For a 9-patch grid, which needs three equal divisions, go to 12″ again, but this time make a mark every 4″ (5–17).

For a 36-square grid with six equal divisions, 12″ will still work, but this time make a mark every 2″ (5–18).

For a 25–square grid with five equal divisions, go to 12½″ and make a mark every 2½″ (5–19).

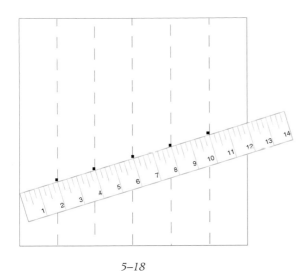

5–18

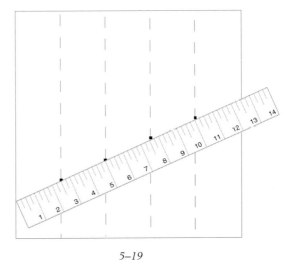

5–19

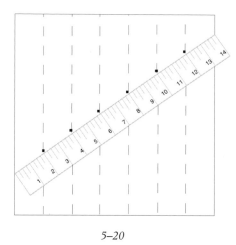

5–20

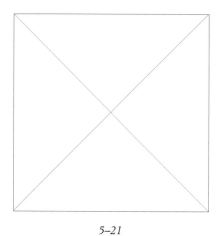

5–21

For a 49-square grid with seven equal divisions, go to 14″ and make a mark every 2″ (5–20).

Depending on the size of the square you are working with, you may find a metric ruler more useful. All you are looking for is a certain number of *equal* divisions that end up *longer* than the width of the square. Sometimes metric measurements are better, and sometimes inch measurements are better. In fact, I have used this method simply by counting off divisions on lined paper and angling the paper across the square just as I would a ruler.

The *Eight-Pointed Star* grid is completely different than the grids based on a series of equal squares. What is needed for this grid is a series of equal angles radiating outward from the center. Then, when those lines hit the sides of the square, other lines for the grid can be drawn. Once again there are several ways to get the grid, and I am always learning new ones. The method described below is one of the latest I have discovered. There are several illustrations in this sequence and, for clarity, the lines in each new addition to the drawing are designated in red.

Begin by drawing an *accurate* square in the size you need and, using a ruler, draw diagonal lines from corner to corner (5–21).

Next, place a right-angle (90°) triangle along the bottom edge of the square and line it up to the point in the center of the square where the diagonal lines cross (5–22). Draw the line dividing the square in half. Turn the square and, once again, using the right-angle triangle, draw the line in the other direction (5–23).

In order to complete the grid, there needs to be one more set of lines exactly between each of the lines radiating from the center. First draw a square within the square by connecting the midpoints of the square as shown in Illustration 5–24.

Place the point of a compass in the exact center of the square and open the compass until it exactly hits the midpoint of the side of the square. Lightly draw the circle within the square. The circle should exactly fit within the square as shown in Illustration 5–25.

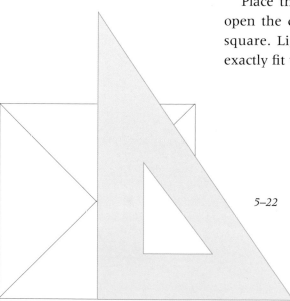

5–22

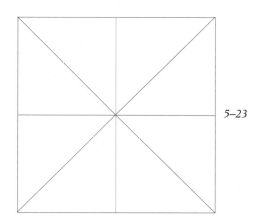

5–23

The place where the circle crosses the diagonal lines to the corners is the reference point for drawing another square as shown in 5–26.

Finally, the place where the two squares within the larger square cross (marked with green dots in Illustration 5–26) is the reference point for drawing the final set of lines coming from the center of the block. Place a ruler from one of these points, bringing it *through the center of the square* to the same point on the opposite side. Draw the line, and repeat the process for the other three lines (5–27 and 5–28).

These last lines hit the edge of the square at the places where the points of the *Eight-Pointed Star* would fall. I have marked those points alternately with green and purple dots going clockwise around the square. Connect every green dot to a purple dot, and you will have the basic *Eight-Pointed Star* grid (5–29a).

Erase the circle, unless you plan on using this grid later for a *Mariner's Compass* type design (5–29b), and leave the two inner squares or erase them (5–29c). For more complicated designs, the more lines the better,

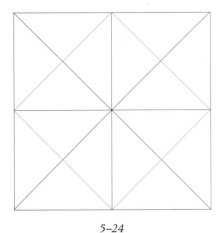

5–24

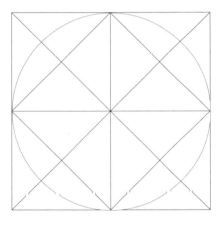

5–25

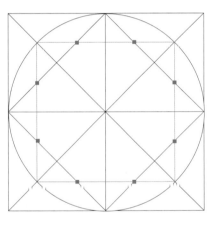

5–26

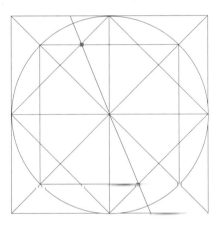

5–27

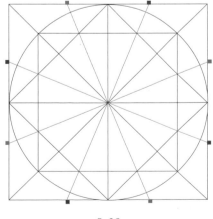

5–28

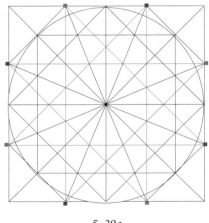

5–29a

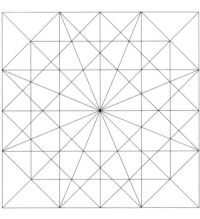

5–29b

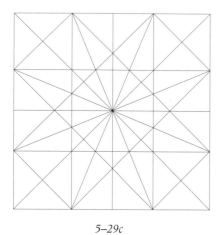

5–29c

but for simpler ones, the lines might get confusing. Illustration 5–29c is the basic *Eight-Pointed Star* grid that I use most of the time.

While it is a little more difficult to recognize which designs fall into the *Eight-Pointed Star* category, with practice these patterns can become as easy to draft as ones in the other categories.

My 20 original designs plus the five other blocks illustrated throughout this book are presented again here, but now they are grouped by category (5–30 to 5–32). There is a subtle blue grid under each block so that you can see how the grid was used to draft each one. In some cases, it is necessary to draw some of the lines of the design to the midpoint of the grid, in essence dividing each square in half. Where this is necessary, *red* lines indicate the further breakdown of the grid.

I hope that the foregoing explanation and the following designs with the grids under them will enable you to draft any of the patterns in this book in any size you wish.

Nine-Patch, 36-Square Grid Designs

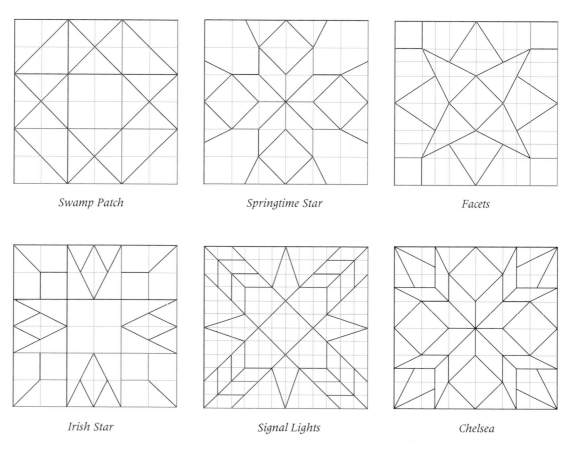

Swamp Patch

Springtime Star

Facets

Irish Star

Signal Lights

Chelsea

5–30

Four-Patch, 64-Square Grid Designs

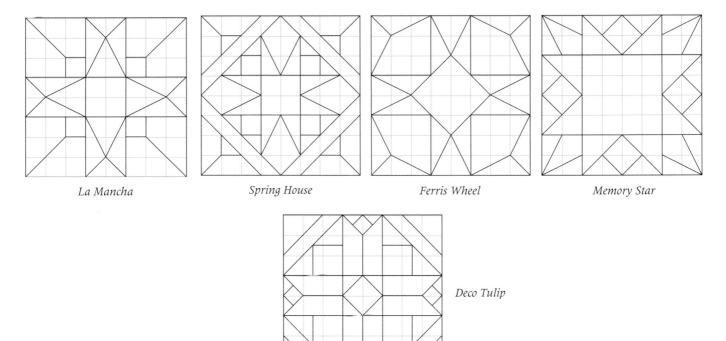

La Mancha

Spring House

Ferris Wheel

Memory Star

Deco Tulip

Five-Patch, 25-Square Grid Designs

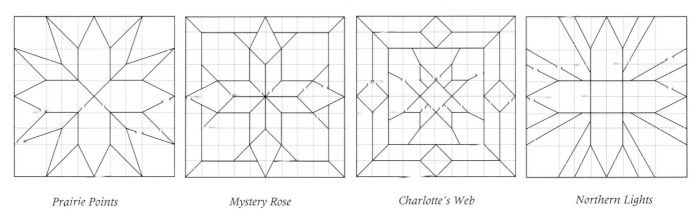

Prairie Points

Mystery Rose

Charlotte's Web

Northern Lights

Seven-Patch, 49-Square Grid Designs

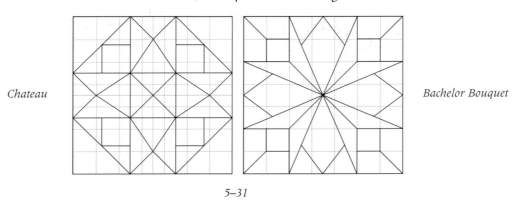

Chateau

Bachelor Bouquet

5–31

Eight-Pointed Star Grid Design

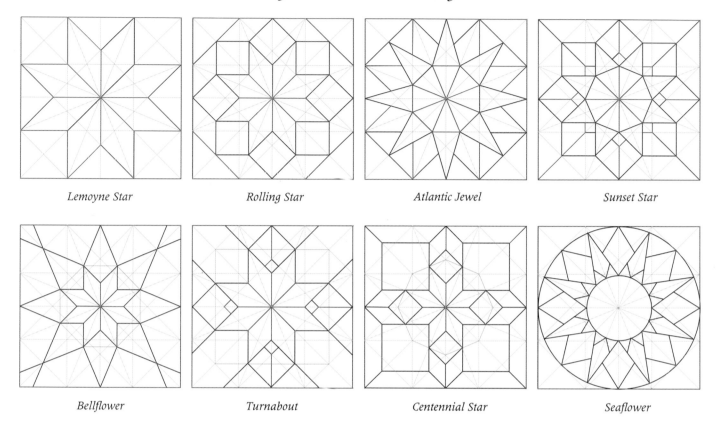

Lemoyne Star   Rolling Star   Atlantic Jewel   Sunset Star

Bellflower   Turnabout   Centennial Star   Seaflower

5–32

MAKING TEMPLATES

Templates are the patterns that are used to cut out the pieces from fabric. If the template is not accurate, the piecing will not be accurate. A transparent plastic material is preferable for making templates, particularly for the soft-edge technique, as it enables you to see through the template and center portions of the fabric design within the shape.

When cutting pieces from fabric, you must add a seam allowance to all sides of all pieces. Traditionally, quilters use a 1/4" seam allowance. There are typically two ways in which most people add the seam allowance. Some cut the template the exact size of the finished piece, draw around the template onto the wrong side of the fabric, then arbitrarily cut out from that line an approximate 1/4". This is done so the pencil line can be used as a guide for sewing the pieces together. Others add an exact 1/4" to the template, cut the fabric pieces that size, and then either "eyeball" the 1/4" when sewing, or mark the 1/4" later. I prefer the latter and feel compelled to get on my soapbox for a minute to give you the reasons.

When the sewing line is marked and the seam allowance is arbitrarily cut out from that line, I believe that it takes more than twice as much time to hand-piece a block—at least for me, it does. First of all, the cutting takes almost twice as long because each piece in the block must be individually cut. If a motif from the fabric is not to be centered, two pieces at a time can safely be cut without any loss of accuracy.

Second, when two pieces are put together to begin sewing, a lot of time is spent carefully pinning and making sure that the sewing lines are together, whereas if you have added an exact seam allowance, all that is necessary is to line up the cut edges, pin them together, and begin sewing.

The actual sewing part also takes longer because you have to keep checking the back side of the work to make sure the pieces are still together and that you are sewing directly on the line both front and back. Also, when you are finished with the block, it is necessary to trim all the seams because some of them may have been cut too wide and might interfere with the quilting.

For those people who feel they need the security of having a line to sew on, I recommend putting tiny holes in the template right along the seam line. The most important places for these holes are at the points where the seam allowances would meet, but more can be added if desired. Then, when ready to sew, place two pieces together matching the cut edges, and pin them in place. Put the template on top of the piece that will be facing you as you sew, and put pencil marks through the holes onto the fabric. Then you can sew dot to dot.

➥ NOTE: *One easy way to put the holes into the plastic template is to fold an old towel several times and place the template on top of it. Then, with a small knitting needle, tapestry needle, or other sharp object, poke holes into the template along the seam line. By poking the holes into the plastic in this manner, a rough surface will appear on the underside of the template. This is helpful for holding the template securely to the fabric when drawing around it in preparation for cutting. A $1/8$" or $1/16$" hole punch is also useful for cutting the holes.*

To actually make the template, place the transparent plastic directly on the pattern over each shape. Place a ruler on the plastic along the edge of the shape. (A metal ruler with cork on the back is ideal as it is less likely to slip.)

Mark along the edge of the shape (the sewing line), and then add $1/4$" to that. There is a great tool called a Dritz® Quilter's Disk that I like to use for adding the $1/4$". It is a small metal disk with a hole in the middle that is exactly $1/4$" from the edge. Without moving the ruler from the edge of the shape, place the disk right next to the ruler, put a sharp pencil through the hole, and draw along the ruler. This will add an exact

¼" to the template. Repeat for each side of the template. If you do not have or cannot find such a tool, use a see-through gridded ruler, place it along the edge of the shape with ¼" going beyond the edge and draw the ¼".

Templates for the soft-edge pieces will be made the same. When drawing around the fabric on those pieces, mark along the template edges where the shape will be pieced, but cut ⅛" out from the *motif* on the fabric where the piece will be appliquéd. The reason for only ⅛" seam allowance for appliqué versus the ¼" for piecing is that when turning the fabric under for appliqué, it is easier to get a smooth edge with the smaller allowance.

WASHING THE FABRIC

Wash all fabric before using it in your quilts. This will eliminate any residual shrinkage, make the fabric softer—and therefore easier to sew. Most important, it will wash out excess dye and make darker colors less apt to run later.

If you have bright or dark colors that you want to use with lighter colors follow these steps. Soak the fabric for at least an hour in cold water to help "set" the dyes. Next, wash the fabric in cold water with a phosphate-free detergent. (Detergents with phosphates cause a fabric to bleed more readily.) Watch the rinse water carefully, and if a lot of color comes out in the water, wash the fabric *again* with a piece of white or muslin-colored cloth. After the wash, check to see if the light cloth was contaminated with color from the other fabric. If it was, do not use the colored fabric with very light colors. If not, it should be safe to use. Never wash bright or dark-colored fabric or quilts made with them in hot water.

It should be noted that dye will run from some fabrics, but will *not* stain others, yet other fabrics may have dye run from them that *will* stain others. This is why it is best to use the "white cloth" test.

To avoid having fabrics run later after they are pieced into a block, there are several precautions to keep in mind. The *most* important is to refrain from leaving excess water sitting in your blocks or quilts. *This means any time you wash them, even if by hand, put them into your washing machine to spin out any excess water.* If you have used one of those water soluble marking pens (which I would *never* do), do not spritz the block with water and allow it to dry. The water will be sitting in the fabric too long and might cause running to occur. Use a permanent press setting when ironing your blocks. Too hot an iron can cause certain types of dyes to melt and run into adjacent fabrics.

If you have had a problem with bleeding, wash the quilt or blocks *again* on a gentle cycle for just a few minutes in the largest load possible (to have plenty of water in relation to the quilt or blocks) with *cold* water and a phosphate-free detergent. Very often, the discoloration will come out in the wash.

CUTTING

Before cutting out the block, it is important to consider where the grain line will be on each of the pieces. On the soft-edge shapes, the grain will be determined by the design on the fabric, but particular attention should be paid to the other pieces.

The lengthwise grain of the fabric runs the length of the goods, the crosswise grain runs from selvage to selvage, and the bias is the diagonal of the fabric. Wherever possible, I like to have the lengthwise grain or alternately the crosswise grain, running along the outer edges of the finished block. When the block is broken down into units, I also like to have the grain of the fabric running along the outer edges of each unit.

Try to avoid having bias edges fall on the outside of the block, as this will cause the edges to stretch, and the block will become distorted. For example, even though the triangles on the *Eight-Pointed Star* block shown here are identical, they would be cut differently for the block. The two short sides of the corner triangles would be cut on the lengthwise and crosswise grain since that is the outside edge. The triangle in the middle of the block's sides would be cut with its *long* side along the grain line (5–33).

For 45° diamonds and *Mariner's Compass* points and wedges, I put the

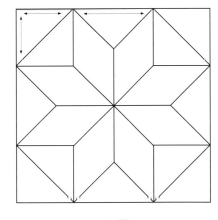

5–33

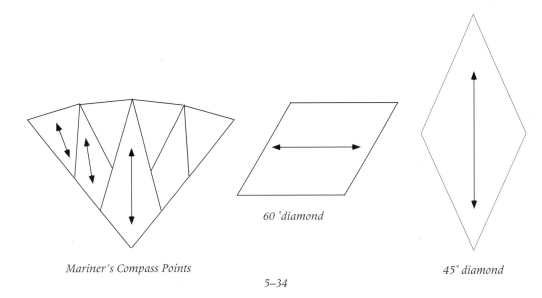

Mariner's Compass Points

60°diamond

45° diamond

5–34

straight grain up the middle of the shape, but for 60° diamonds, I have it running along two parallel edges. The arrows on the illustrations here indicate where I would place the grain when cutting the pieces (5–34).

It is safe to cut two pieces at a time. The fabric can be folded together and will be less apt to slip if it is pressed lightly with an iron. If a motif from the fabric is to be placed in a particular spot within the shape, then each piece will have to be cut individually.

It is important to be extremely accurate when marking around the template and cutting out the pieces. A piece of tailor's chalk honed to a fine edge can give a good mark that is easy to see. A pencil does not mark as easily and tends to drag on the fabric, which might cause some distortion. It is also difficult to see on dark fabrics.

I most often use a ball-point pen to mark around templates. Before you are too quick to condemn me for this blasphemous act, let me explain. I always add an exact ¼″ seam allowance to templates; then, after marking the cutting line, I cut just *inside* the pen line, so no pen mark remains on the fabric. The pen glides smoothly over the fabric, does not drag, and is visible on most fabrics. I would *never* mark with a pen if that was a sewing line, and I would *never* mark quilting motifs with a pen. If I were to cut holes in the template and mark dots for sewing guides (as explained previously), I would *not* use a pen, but a pencil because the mark would remain on the fabric.

HAND APPLIQUÉ

There are many ways to appliqué. I prefer the ones given here for the soft-edge technique, but if you have another favorite method, you should do what makes you most comfortable.

Most of the soft-edge pieces you have cut will probably have some sort of line along the edge of the motif, which will be appliquéd. I start with the right side of the soft-edge piece *facing* me and carefully turn to the back the ⅛″ turn-under allowance, leaving the line showing. I fold the edge toward the back, baste it down with a simple running stitch, and leave the beginning knot of the thread on *top*. Instead of making a knot at the end, I leave about a 4″-long "tail" hanging.

After the edge is basted under, I carefully press the piece with the right side facing up, making sure that the edges are smooth. Next, the soft-edge piece is placed on the background or base, pinned carefully in place, and then basted securely to the background. Once again, the beginning knot of the basting thread is on top of the work, and no knot is used at the end.

Finally the piece is appliquéd in place with the same color thread as the piece being appliquéd. If there is a line around the edge of the motif, use thread the color of the line. When the appliqué is complete, take hold of the knots and carefully pull out the basting threads.

THE STITCH

To appliqué, use a standard-weight 100%-cotton sewing thread. Work with a size needle you feel is comfortable. My preference is to use a very small #12 "between" needle. To thread such a small needle, pull the thread from the spool, hold it taut, then cut it off at an angle with very sharp scissors. Angling the thread in this way enables it to go through the eye of the needle much easier than a bluntly cut thread. A needle-threader is another option.

The stitches in Illustration 5–35 have been exaggerated so that you can see the placement of the needle. You should strive to make your stitches as invisible as possible. Using a single-strand thread cut no longer than 18", bring the needle up from underneath about ¼" into the edge of the piece being appliquéd. Going back into the same hole, run the needle *between* the two layers of fabric right to the edge of the soft-edge piece, and come out on top right at the edge. (The reason for doing this is so the knot of the thread will not be at the edge of the appliqué, but well back where it would not be apt to show through the background fabric.)

Next, put the needle down into the background piece directly *below* where the thread comes out of the top piece (5–35). Bring the needle underneath approximately ¹⁄₁₆", and come up through both layers into the *edge* of the top piece. Once again, go down into the background directly below the point where you came out into the top piece. Continue until all is appliquéd. The main consideration is that the stitch is on the *back* of the work and only a small thread is visible, if at all, on the top.

5–35

BRODERIE PERSE STYLE APPLIQUÉ

Broderie perse is a type of appliqué that was popular in quiltmaking during the late-18th and early-19th centuries. Flowers, leaves, birds, branches, and other motifs were cut from a decorative fabric and sewn to a background to create part of the design of the quilt.

The *broderie perse* technique was used in three quilts shown in this chapter. Margaret Smith combines the use of border prints, soft-edge piecing, and *broderie perse* in her medallion quilt, *Summer's Splendor,* shown below. The symmetry of the quilt is enhanced by the repeat of the various elements throughout.

Marjorie Lydecker combined *broderie perse,* soft-edge, and patchwork techniques in *Autumn Album* shown on the facing page. A particularly

P5–1. Summer's Splendor, *made by Margaret Smith, is a medallion quilt incorporating the use of border prints, appliqué, and the soft-edge technique.*

P5–2. Autumn Album, *made by Marjorie Lydecker, is a medallion quilt of appliqué album blocks with pieced and soft-edge borders.*

P5–3. *Detail of signature square on the back of* Autumn Album, *made by Marjorie Lydecker.*

nice finish to this spectacular quilt is the soft-edge signature square on the back of the quilt (P5–3). This photograph also gives you a detailed view of how the peacock was cut from the fabric for the *broderie perse*.

Marjorie Lydecker also used elements of *broderie perse* in her quilt *Indian Summer* shown below where she appliquéd a branch with flowers and a bird in each corner.

In the *broderie perse* technique, sometimes the edges on the motifs are cut beyond the design about ¼" to smooth out any unevenness and

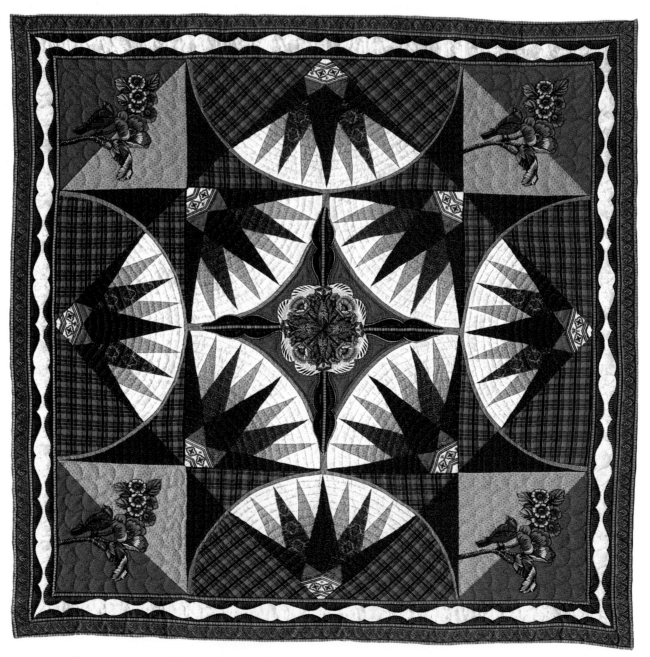

P5–4. Indian Summer, *made by Marjorie Lydecker, is a quilt combining soft-edge borders,* broderie perse, *and piecing.*

then turned under and appliquéd, but in the old quilts, more often than not, the edges were not turned under and the pieces were sewn down with a fine buttonhole stitch. There may be times when the edges of fabric to be used for the soft edge are too detailed to be able to turn under neatly for appliqué. In those instances the *broderie perse* technique using the buttonhole stitch would work well.

In this technique no edges are sewn under, but the buttonhole stitches are so close together that the edges of the fabric will not fray. Even so, through handling while stitching, every now and then small threads may come loose. To eliminate the problem, I like to treat the edges before sewing them down with a product called Fray Check™. If you would like to try this, working on a piece of paper towel, place the piece of fabric upside down, and run a few drops of Fray Check around the edges. Then, with forefinger and thumb, gently run your fingers around the edges spreading the Fray Check evenly and allowing the front side to become slightly moistened as well. Place the pieces on the paper towel and allow them to dry.

When the pieces are dry, place them on the background, carefully baste them about ¼" from the edges, and then sew them down with fine buttonhole stitches. The thread to use is a matter of personal preference depending on how distinct you want the stitches to look. I would recommend a thread no lighter in weight than quilting thread but heavier, if you prefer—such as buttonhole twist, fine perle cotton, embroidery floss, or silk thread.

There are various methods of sewing a buttonhole stitch. When I began my quilt *Olde World Star*, I researched and tried different techniques, but the one I liked the best came from *The Needleworker's Dictionary* by Pamela Clabburn. In it, she describes how to make a double-beaded edge instead of the normal single-beaded edge. "With the edge to be worked facing away, the needle is brought up from underneath and the thread drawn through until only a small loop is left. The needle is then put through the loop from behind and the thread drawn tight." The only difference that I make to this description is that I like to hold the edge to be worked facing toward my right and then work down toward myself as in Illustration 5–36. What I like best about this technique is that it leaves a nice neat ridge of knots on the top of the stitches. On the next page is a detailed photograph (P5–5) of the *broderie perse* technique done in my quilt *Olde World Star*.

➥ N O T E : *You may find as you appliqué that after a few stitches, the thread begins to twist and eventually knot. When this begins to happen, take hold of the end of the thread and pull the needle down all the way to the fabric. Let go of the thread and then slowly pull the needle back up to the position you want it for sewing. Pulling the needle up in this fashion will untwist the thread and you will be able to take several more stitches before the thread begins to twist again.*

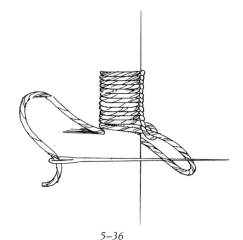

5–36

P5–5. Detail, Olde World Star.

HAND PIECING

How you piece your patches together is a matter of personal preference. Some people use only the sewing machine, some only sew by hand, and others do both. I hand-piece all of my quilts. Many people are aghast at this and wonder how I have the time, how much patience I must have, and why don't I use the machine.

To me the enjoyment I get from patchwork and quilting is the process. I don't do it to have an immediately finished product, but to have something to do with my *hands*. I'm the kind of person who has to be doing *something* with my hands. My husband knows if I ever sit in front of the TV doing nothing, I must be sick or very tired.

I began sewing at the age of 5, made my own clothes starting at age 12, and made draperies, my clothes, and the children's clothes in adulthood. The sewing machine was for producing products *fast*; it was for cutting out a dress one day and finishing it the next. But through all of this, I always had hand projects—embroidery, knitting, crochet—that could be done in "spare" time or "relax" time. When quilting came along, it was a relax-time activity. I didn't want to take away from the joy of having something to do when I relaxed by doing it quickly on the machine and then having nothing to do with my hands when I was ready to sit quietly. Furthermore, after a busy day when I could finally sit down of an evening and relax, I wouldn't want to go to the sewing machine but would rather sit quietly with my husband and family and either watch TV or listen to music and have some handwork to do.

There is so much "found time" available. People say to me that it takes so much *patience* to hand-piece, but I become *impatient* if I have to stand in line, wait at a doctor's office, wait for my computer to "think," be delayed at an airport, or be a passenger in a car with no handwork to do. With my lifestyle, it would take longer to machine-piece than to hand-piece. It takes blocks of time to sit at the sewing machine, and I never seem to have those blocks of time. When I do have time is during those moments of "found" time or in the evening when I just want to relax. All of my life, I have equated the sewing machine with "work," and while something could be done quickly on the machine, for me, it was never relaxing.

The secret to getting a lot of handwork done is to always have something available to sew on, something that can be picked up in those "found" moments. I keep a phone by my quilting frame and I keep hand-piecing at each other phone. When I get a call, I usually start sewing or quilting immediately. I try to have sewing in my purse so that I can pick it up at various odd moments when I am away from the house,

THE SEWING

To begin sewing, study the design to determine the order of piecing. Try to have straight seams wherever possible. For example, to sew four squares together, first sew two patches, then the other two patches and finally join the two sections together with one long seam (5–37).

For designs such as *Irish Star* and *Bachelor Bouquet*, individual units

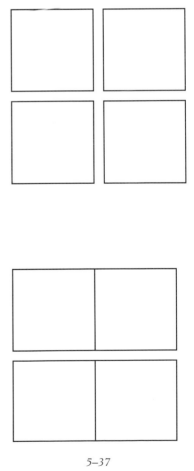

5–37

would be sewn first, then the units sewn together in sections, and finally the sections sewn together with one long straight seam (5–38 and 5–39).

The size needle to use for handpiecing is a matter of personal preference. I like to use a very small needle, a "between" #12, but I look for a brand where the needle is very sturdy. I use a heavy-duty 100%-cotton thread cut no longer than 18" in length and usually a neutral-colored thread that blends with both pieces being sewn together. When sewing a very light-colored fabric to a dark one, the stitches are less apt to show if the thread color matches the darkest fabric being sewn.

I begin sewing with a knot at the end of the thread. There are various

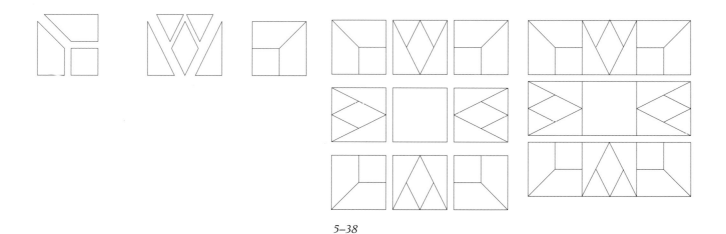

5–38

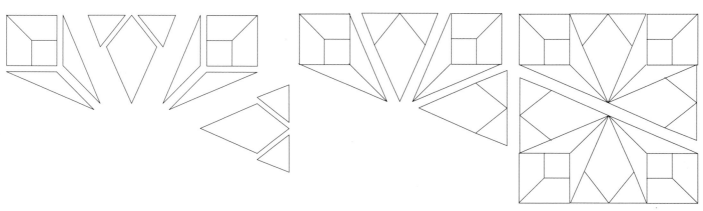

5–39

ways to make the knot. Some people begin with a backstitch, others wrap the thread around the needle several times, then pull the needle through, which leaves the knot at the end. The knot I use is made by wrapping the end of the thread around the forefinger a couple of times, then pushing it off the finger with the thumb, twisting it as I push. Then I grab the thread between the fingernails of my thumb and forefinger, and pull down to form the knot.

Assuming that you have added an exact ¼" seam allowance to your templates, pin the first two pieces together with the raw edges matching. If you do not feel you can "eyeball" a ¼" seam, place the template from which the piece facing you was cut on top of the piece and lightly mark dots through the holes. Then sew the ¼" seam by taking small running stitches. I get as many stitches on the needle as I can, almost like a small gathering stitch, then every time I come up, I will take a small backstitch before continuing the gathering motion.

The knot I make when finished stitching is done by making a backstitch, pulling the needle almost all the way through until only a small loop is left, and then putting the needle through the loop and pulling the thread all the way up.

Probably the most common problem in piecing is getting corners to match. One secret to matching corners has already been discussed, and that is to piece in units with straight seams wherever possible. The other secret is to make sure that the sewing at the joints of seams and corners is very tight. Seams that match perfectly when you sew them can shift if they are not sewn tightly enough where the corners meet. One of the best ways to keep the joining of the seams tight is to keep the seams free when handsewing. Sewing across the seams results in a lot of excess bulk at the corners, making it impossible to get the stitching tight enough.

When joining four seams, I stitch two pieces together and then the other two. Next, I pin the two together with the seams on one going one direction and the seams on the other going the other direction. This produces a small ridge on each piece that can nestle right next to the other. As I approach the place where the seams join, I carefully remove the pin, making sure the ridges are still abutting each other. Then I carefully lift the seams up and sew directly to the seam line making sure I am not sewing into the seams themselves. I take a backstitch, pulling the thread tight, then pass the needle through the base of the seam to the other side, pulling the thread tight. I do a backstitch again to make sure the seam is very tight and continue sewing across. I follow the same process no matter how many points are to be sewn together by first sewing two halves then joining the halves with one straight seam across.

Chapter 6

PLANNING THE QUILT

For me, making a quilt is sort of like taking a walk in the woods. You know where you are going, but don't know for sure everything you will see along the way. I begin a quilt with a basic outline, but how all the spaces will be filled are decisions to be made along the way. To help you understand the process, I will take you through the steps that I used when making my quilt, *Olde World Star* shown on the next page.

SELECTING THE BLOCK AND PLANNING OVERALL DESIGN

I began by designing the basic block, which was based on an *Eight-Pointed Star* with a smaller star in the inner octagon. Both the small and large stars have another set of points between each of the main points. I then studied the block to determine where soft edges might be effective, decided to change the secondary points on both stars to a soft edge, and drew a line drawing of the block with the soft edges sketched in.

DETERMINING VALUE PLACEMENT

Next came determining where dark, medium, and light values would fall within the block. Using a black marker, I filled the shapes with various shades of black to gray, photocopied it several times, and then put the copies together to see what the design would look like. With all the blocks together, it seemed that something had to be done in the large space created where the corners of the blocks joined. I decided to begin making stars and that perhaps after some of the stars were complete, they would help to dictate what should happen in that space.

P6–1. Olde World Star, *made by the author.*

CHOOSING COLORS

The next step was to select the colors and fabrics that were to be used in the quilt. Here, a brief synopsis of the system I use for selecting a color scheme is in order. (For a complete explanation of the color system I use, refer to *Color Confidence for Quilters,* listed in the bibliography.)

My basic philosophy is that *any* colors can be used together. It is not the initial colors chosen that are important, but what is put with them that makes them work. Make sure that there is always a very *dark* (a color darker than all the others), and an *accent* (a brighter version of one of the colors). Finally, if those chosen colors can be shaded together, you will always have a nice combination. Shading in this way forces you to add colors you might never have thought of using, and takes the palette from ordinary to unusual. Think of how a rainbow looks. The colors blend beautifully together with it almost impossible to tell where one color ends and the next one begins. Try to do the same with the colors you select, adding whatever other colors are needed to subtly shade from one to the next.

The three easiest ways to approach shading the colors together are to go darker and darker with two colors until they blend together through black, or to go lighter and lighter connecting through very light, or to blend through medium tones.

Many people select a fabric that particularly appeals to them to use for developing a color scheme. Often there is disappointment because they choose colors that exactly match the colors in their original fabric and then wonder why, when the quilt is done, that something seems to be missing. Very often they miss seeing the very dark outline that defines and delineates areas of the pattern in the fabric. That same very dark color, if missing in the quilt, will cause the overall effect to be flat. Furthermore, when selecting only colors that exactly match the colors in the original fabric, the accent may be missing because there will be no color just a little brighter than the others.

Beginning with a fabric that appeals to you for establishing a color scheme is a great approach, particularly if you have found a wonderful fabric with soft-edge capabilities. But don't stop at selecting only the colors in the print for your palette. Select those colors, but then *add* all the other shades and hues necessary to blend from one color to another (6–1), and you will have a great color scheme every time!

The approach described above is the one I used for selecting the color scheme for my quilt, *Olde World Star.* I began with the border, found fabrics in the colors that matched the ones found in the border print and then selected the colors I needed to blend all of the original ones together. Illustration 6–1 shows the border print, the exact match colors (at the

6–1

bottom), and the complete shaded palette. You can see how I shaded from the turquoise into teal, then to green and darker with the green until it flowed into black. From there I went to very dark brown and into burgundy, through reds, terra cotta, into peach and finally to beige and very light. The palette is for color only. I used many *different* prints in those colors to give a variety in the textures that were used. In fact, the quilt contains more than 40 different fabrics. I searched specifically for fabrics that would have soft-edge possibilities.

DECIDING WHERE TO USE THE FABRICS WITHIN THE BLOCK

The next step for me was to look again at the black-and-white shaded version of the design and to determine where the various colors and fabrics would go. The border print would always be used in the center of the block, and a tiny border would always outline the octagon, which contains the small star. The points of the center star would always be dark green, and I would shade the points of each large star from peach through red and finally to very dark green. I would always do the soft-edge technique coming from behind the points of both the small and large stars and had originally planned on using different fabrics in each star for that technique.

Using the same general colors and shading, I decided to make each star different, and with as many *different* fabrics as possible. Furthermore, because I wasn't exactly sure what would be best for the soft edge behind the large stars or for the background that would be used, I decided to just sew stars for a while and make those decisions later.

Each of the blocks contained a different technique for the soft-edge motif behind the points of the small stars. Some were turned under and appliquéd, but others had such uneven edges that I laid them flat and did a fine buttonhole stitch in black thread to hold them in place as was described on page 103.

PLANNING THE FINAL DESIGN OF THE QUILT

When the stars were complete, I laid them out onto several different fabrics that could have made a suitable background. Since my plan was to do quite a lot of intricate quilting, a light-colored solid was chosen to

6–2

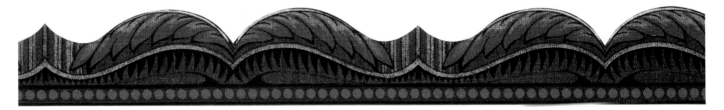

6–3

allow the quilting to stand out as much as possible. But then it seemed to me that, just as the octagon surrounding the small stars was enclosed with a small border print, the points of the large stars needed an outline as well. Furthermore, it was apparent that the large square, which was formed where the points of the stars joined, was very prominent and a design element in itself. To do a different soft-edge motif on each star would disrupt the identity of that large square, because each of its four corners would be different. It was at that point the decision was made to use the *same* fabric for the soft-edge motif behind each of the large stars.

The next decision was to determine the design element for the large square. It was here that I called on the aid of my friend Darlene Christopherson. Together we studied the several possibilities. Since many of the soft-edge motifs in the small star were sewn down with the buttonhole stitch, we thought it might be interesting to cut up flowers and leaves from some of the fabrics I had used and create a bouquet in the middle of the square. I sketched it out, and it seemed like there was a bull's eye in the center of each of the squares.

We finally decided that a smaller square set diagonally within the large square would look good. That small square could have a soft-edge border around the outside and the *broderie perse* bouquet could go in the middle of the smaller squares. On the previous page in Illustration 6–2 is the border print that I had been using for the octagons in the center of each star. Illustration 6–3 shows the piece cut from it that was used for the soft-edge motif around the edges of the squares.

Next, we cut out several leaves and flowers from the various fabrics I had collected and proceeded to create a bouquet. In order to distinguish the small square from the solid background used for the stars, I chose a *different*, slightly darker fabric for the background of the bouquets. Because the edges of the pieces were so uneven, I sewed all the edges down with the buttonhole stitch explained on page 103. On page 104, Photograph P5-5 shows a detail of the technique used in my quilt.

PLANNING THE BORDER

The border is probably one of the most difficult parts of designing a quilt. I never plan a border in advance, but wait until all of the blocks are complete and sewn together. Then I pin the quilt to the cork wall in my work room and try many different combinations of prints and borders of varying widths, until the combination seems right. The main consideration is that the border frames and enhances the rest of the quilt and does not look like something that was tacked on to make the quilt larger. I like to use elements of color, design, and fabric in the border that were used in the rest of the quilt and not introduce anything completely new, unless the general feeling echoes something from the center. Often I will work with a friend when planning a border, because sometimes another eye will see something differently.

For *Olde World Star*, I decided to incorporate into the border the same soft-edge frame and background fabric that was used within the small squares inside the quilt. The inner and outer edges of the border utilized parts of the larger border print that I had been using throughout the quilt—a narrower part on the inside and the wider part on the outside. My preference in addition to having the wider part of the border on the outside is to also have dark toward the outside, so the border was turned so that the darkest part of it was around the outer edge of the quilt and the lighter part toward the inside.

P6–2. Victorian Kaleidoscope, *made by Nancy Johnson, is a quilt top incorporating piecing and soft-edge piecing.*

As you plan borders, echo something in the border that was used inside the quilt, work with varying widths of the various border elements until the proportion seems just right, and use fabrics, colors, and design elements that have already been incorporated into the rest of the quilt.

Marjorie Lydecker used the same border print that I used for *Olde World Star* in both of her quilts, *Autumn Album* and *Indian Summer*, shown on pages 101 and 102. In both quilts, she cut the identical "soft-edge" borders from the fabric, but they look entirely different. In *Autumn Album*, the soft-edge border is used singly, in the center of the quilt and again around the outer edge. In *Indian Summer*, she has used two of those borders facing each other around the outside of the quilt. This border echoes the same motif used for the soft edge in the center of the block.

Margaret Smith used a soft-edge border in several places in her quilt, *Summer's Splendor*, shown on page 100. This beautiful quilt is a perfect example of the balance that can be achieved by repeating elements throughout the quilt.

Nancy Johnson integrated both hard-edge and soft-edge piecing in her quilt top *Victorian Kaleidoscope*, shown on page 115. The circular soft-edge border echoes the soft-edge motif in the center, and the repeat of the hard-line points from the center of the quilt to the outer border adds a nice balance.

The repeated use of the border print in both hard and soft-edge variations, as well as the balance of colors, give continuity to *Eastern Sonrise* (on the facing page) made by Cindy Blackberg. She began with a design in *Patchwork Portfolio* called *Eastern Sunrise*, softened the north, south, east, and west points and then totally changed the look of the design by setting the blocks on point and overlapping the corners. The final border, which includes an accent color from the center and the original border print, complete the design.

Linda Pool began with a paisley fabric, the complete motif of which can be seen in the corners of her quilt, *A Royal Christmas*, shown on page 118. Her fabric supply was limited so she worked with photocopies of the fabric to create the design. When she had several photocopied blocks complete, she determined that to make every block in the soft-edge technique would be too busy. She decided to alternate a soft-edge block with a hard-edge one. She then added to the continuity of the quilt by repeating the points from the hard-edge star as well as a soft motif from the paisley in the final border.

P6–3. Eastern Sonrise, *made by Cindy Blackberg, is a quilt incorporating soft-edge piecing in a traditional-style block.*

P6–4. A Royal Christmas, *made by Linda Pool, is a quilt alternating hard-edge blocks with soft-edge ones.*

THE QUILTING

The quilting is as important to the overall design of a quilt as any other aspect. I consider myself a traditionalist, particularly when it comes to the actual quilting. I like for the quilting to enhance the elements used in the quilt. On patchwork portions of the design, I almost always quilt 1/4" in from the seam around all sides of all pieces. The exception to this is when border prints are used. Then I like to quilt following the design on the border. In *Olde World Star* where eight triangles formed an octagon in the center of each block, I did not want to emphasize the triangles, but rather the design that was formed when the triangles were put together. Therefore, I quilted following the designs formed by the triangles rather than around the triangles themselves. On the portions of the quilt where the soft-edge technique was used between the points of stars, I quilted the background right next to the appliquéd edge, then quilted *following the design on the fabric* on the soft-edge piece itself, following the design in the fabric, as shown in the photographs on page 120.

Small "outline" borders can be a problem. They are usually so narrow that it is impossible to quilt inside of them, but if they are left unquilted, they bulge out and look incomplete. On my quilt I chose to quilt "in the ditch" on either side of the small outline borders. In the ditch means quilting right in the seam on the side that has no extra layers of fabric under it. If this is to be done, you will want to plan in advance and carefully press the seams in those portions of the quilt to one side. Then when quilting, you would quilt just to the other side so that you are not quilting on top of the seam allowances.

It is important to fill all spaces with some kind of quilting. How elaborate that quilting is will be up to you. Look at the detail photograph of the small square with the *broderie perse* bouquet in the center shown on page 104. You will see that the quilting goes around the entire bouquet, as well as around the individual flowers and leaves within the bouquet. At times, when there would have been too large a space left unquilted, I also quilted some of the details within the leaves and flowers.

I quilted following the design in the fabric on the soft-edge border in the small squares and then right next to the soft-edge border on the background fabric, finishing by echo quilting at 1/4" intervals until the quilting lines ran into the bouquet. For balance, the same echo quilting was used outward from the soft edge in the border of the quilt as well.

The light-colored solid background portions of the quilt were very important to me, and I wanted to plan a more elaborate motif for those areas. I drew the square and sketched the two soft-edge pieces on either side, and then created a quilting design that would fill the space, leaving no more than ¼" between the design and the edge of the block. Here it is important to talk about *finishing* the quilting. Often a feather wreath or other decorative quilting design is planned, and once that is quilted into the quilt, no other quilting is done. I think it is important to quilt the area *behind* the motif as well. Furthermore, sometimes the quilting can be enhanced even further by quilting a *double* row of stitches ¹/₁₆" to ¹/₈" apart. Look below at the three detailed photographs of the quilting design in *Olde World Star*. The first one shows the decorative motif only with no other quilting, the second shows the decorative motif with the background quilted in straight rows ³/₁₆" apart, and the third shows the addition of a second line of stitching around the decorative motif. It is this third variation that I chose to use throughout the quilt.

P6–5

P6–6

Details of quilting motif from Olde World Star, *made by the author, showing how different the motif can look depending on the amount of quilting that is done.*

P6–7

Chapter 7

DESIGNS AND PATTERNS

Twenty-five patchwork designs have been used throughout this book for the illustrations, drafting instructions, and exercises. Three of them, *Eight-Pointed Star*, *Rolling Star*, and *Swamp Patch*, are traditional designs, which have been used by quilters for years. Two of the designs, *Atlantic Jewel* and *Spring House*, are my original designs and were first published in *Patchwork Portfolio* in 1989. The other 20 designs are ones I have designed since *Patchwork Portfolio* was published. They were chosen to be used here because I thought they offered particularly good opportunities for the soft-edge technique.

Two of the 20 new designs, *Facets* and *Sunset Star*, were used earlier in the illustrations and are shown in color on pages 49–51 and 84–85. The remainder are shown in color in both hard-edge and soft-edge variations on the following pages. The line drawing of the designs not given as patterns can be found on page 79. Please bear in mind that the renditions here are only *one* way of applying the soft-edge technique to the design. There are many other possibilities that could be used for each design depending on personal preference and choice of fabrics. Remember the *Eight-Pointed Star* and *Rolling Star* examples shown earlier and how many different variations were applied to each one; then have fun experimenting on your own with the designs here.

Patterns are given for eight of the original designs as well as the basic *Eight-Pointed Star* and *Rolling Star*. Unless otherwise noted the patterns are all 11″. Approximately one fourth of each pattern has been given in its entirety. This is to enable you to combine pieces or change the design to accommodate the soft-edge technique.

If you wish to make one of the designs not given here as a pattern, or would like your design to be a different size than the one given here, you will be able to draft your own pattern in whatever size you want by following the drafting instructions on pages 85–94.

To make templates, place a piece of transparent template material over the design and draw each pattern piece that you need for your particular rendition of the design. *Remember to add ¹/4″ seam allowance around all sides of all templates.*

Because the soft-edge technique is so individual, the amount of yardage required is totally dependent upon where the soft-edge technique will be used, and the repeat of the fabric design itself. Therefore it would be impossible to give yardage charts. Furthermore, wherever possible I like to use *different* fabrics in each block, varying the color slightly. I find that, because I use many different fabrics in each block, a quarter yard of each fabric is usually sufficient. The exception to this is the border print and whatever fabrics I have chosen for the soft-edge technique.

The blocks and quilts shown on the following pages have been computer generated from scanned images of fabrics. If I were making those quilts in fabric, I would make each block a little different, altering some of the fabrics to give more depth of overall color. For example, in the quilt *Seaflower*, shown on page 130, I would use several different dark purple fabrics for the points, which contain purple, and several different olive prints for the green points. The soft-edge motif would remain constant to give unity.

THE DESIGNS

For the most part, the two variations of each design shown in this chapter have been made with the same fabrics. In each case, the variation on the left shows the hard-edge version, and the one on the right shows the soft-edge style. One of the nice aspects of soft-edge piecing, however, is that it often allows the use of an additional fabric, which can add a new dimension to the color scheme.

Chelsea

Mystery Rose

Northern Lights

Centennial Star

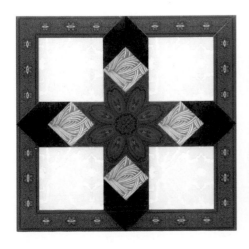

Chateau

Prairie Points

Bachelor Bouquet

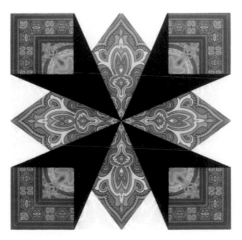 

La Mancha

Deco Tulip

Memory Star

This block was designed as a memory block, where signatures could be written in the space inside the soft-edge central square.

THE PATTERNS

With the exception of *Rolling Star* and *Eight-Pointed Star*, all the patterns here are for an 11″ finished block. At least a quarter section or more is shown so that you will find all of the pieces in each block. A dashed line is used wherever only a partial pattern piece is shown. Some pieces may need to be combined for the soft-edge technique. Therefore, refer to the smaller drawing of the entire block to determine which shapes you will need for your particular soft-edge variation of the block.

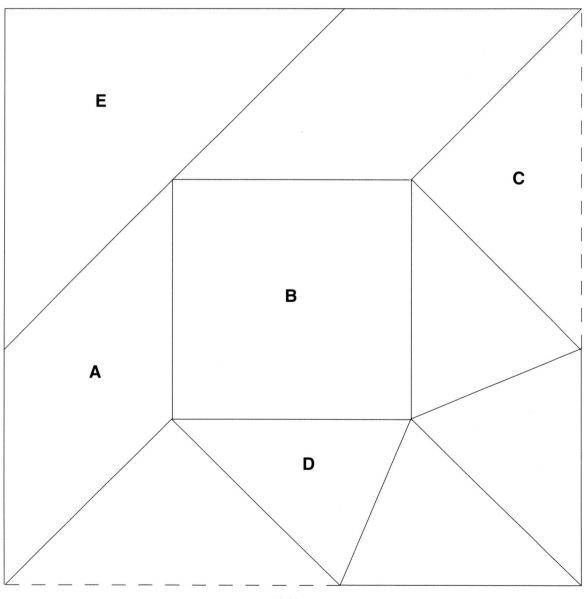

7–21

Rolling Star 12″ and Eight-Pointed Star 8½″

Rolling Star and *Eight-Pointed Star* were used so often in the earlier illustrations that I decided to include a pattern for them here (7–21). Templates made from the portion of the design shown here will produce a 12″ *Rolling Star* and an 8½″ *Eight-Pointed Star*.

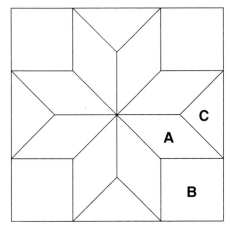

Eight-Pointed Star

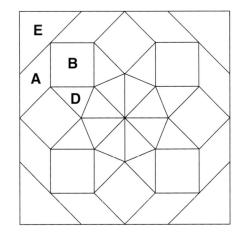

Rolling Star

7–21

Ferris Wheel

The center square was divided into four triangles, which were then cut from a border print for both variations of this design. The soft-edge technique was used between the points of the star and in the corners, which totally changes the look of the design. Compare the hard-edge quilt in Illustration 7–24 to the soft-edge one in Illustration 7–25.

7–22

7–23

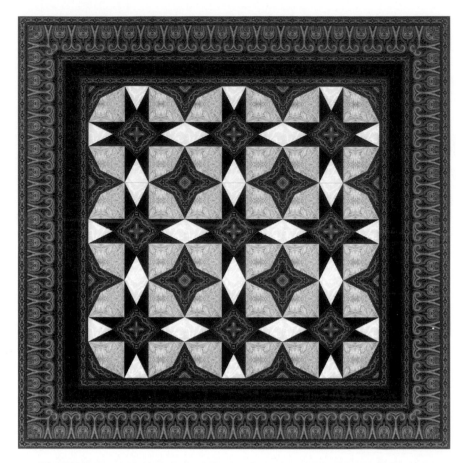

7–24

7–25

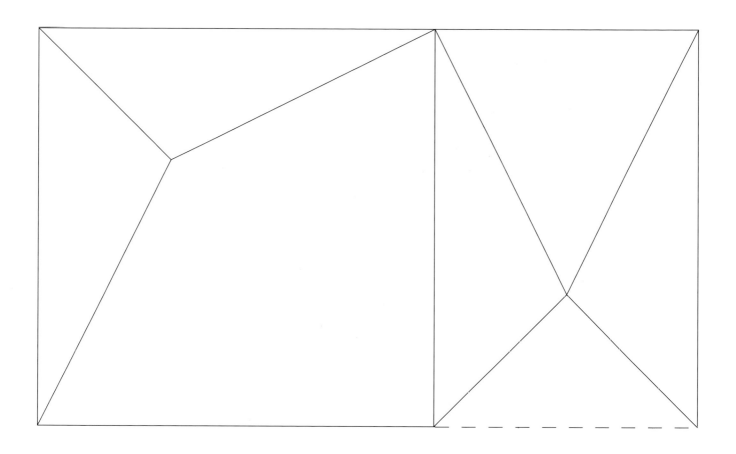

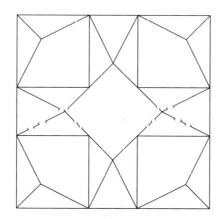

Ferris Wheel

7–26

Seaflower

Only one quarter of the center circle is shown here. Make the full circle by placing the point of a compass at the center of the block and measuring out to the edge of the circle. The addition of the soft-edge technique on the corners helps to fill the spaces between the compasses.

7–27

7–28

7–29

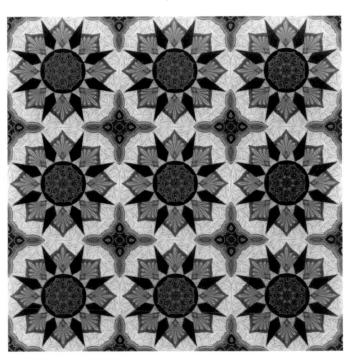

7–30

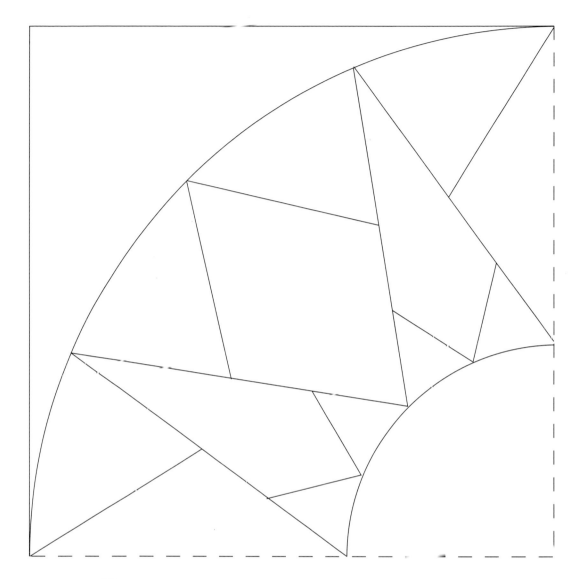

Seaflower

7–31

Turnabout

With the exception of the turquoise "shell" fabric, identical prints were used in both variations of this design. It is hard to imagine that both variations shown here are the same basic design.

7–32

7–33

7–34

7–35

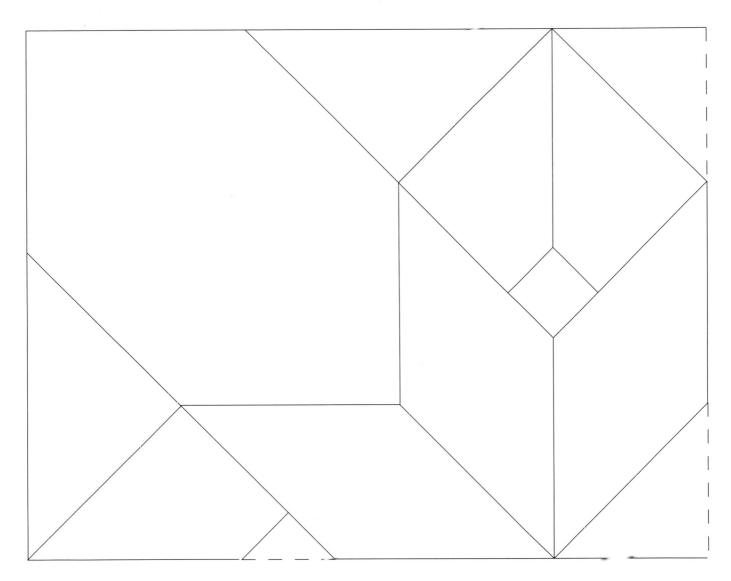

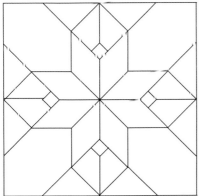

Turnabout

7–36

Charlotte's Web

The hard-edge version of *Charlotte's Web* would do better as a block by itself or alternated with a plain block. It gets very heavy when several are put side-by-side. But adding the soft-edge technique to the inner "border" of the design changes it completely and breaks up the heaviness of the other version.

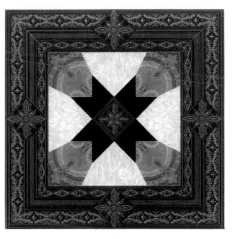

7–37

7–38

7–39

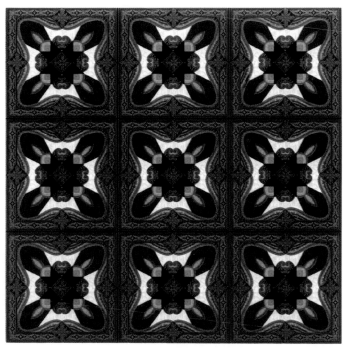

7–40

Charlotte's Web

7–41

Irish Star

Once again, with the exception of the dark purple marble fabric in the soft-edge variation, both blocks have been made with the same fabric. The soft-edge version takes away from the "blockiness" of the hard-edge one.

7–42

7–43

7–44

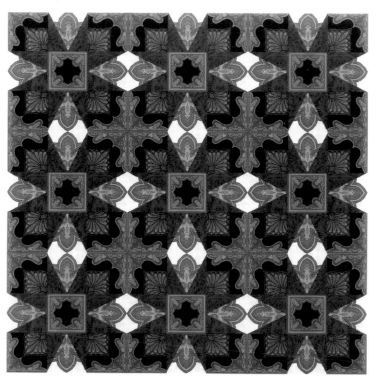

7–45

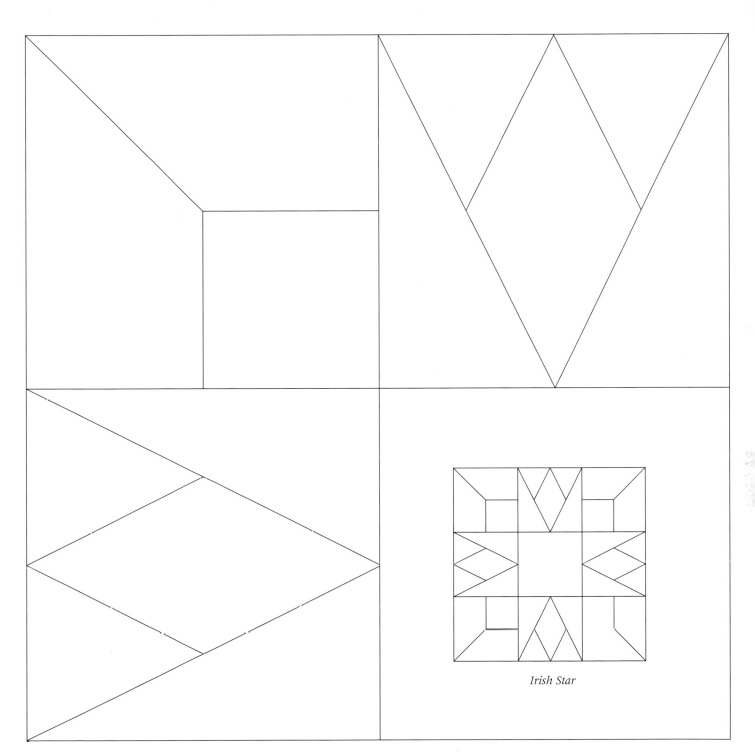

Irish Star

7–46

Bellflower

Bellflower

Three variations of *Bellflower* are shown, one with all hard-edge blocks, one with all soft-edge blocks, and the other alternating the soft-edge blocks with the hard-edge ones as Linda Pool did in her quilt, *A Royal Christmas,* shown on page 118.

7–47

7–48

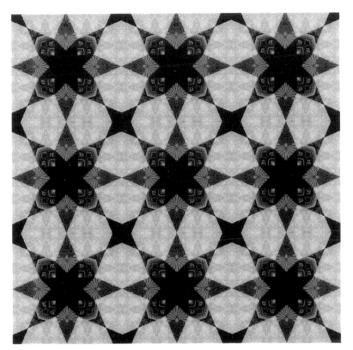

7–49

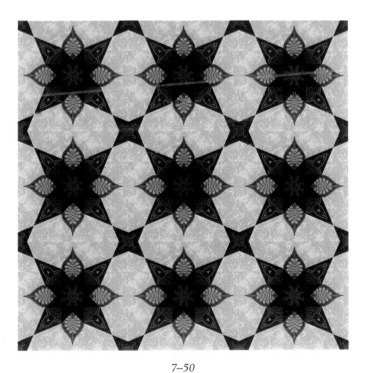

7–50

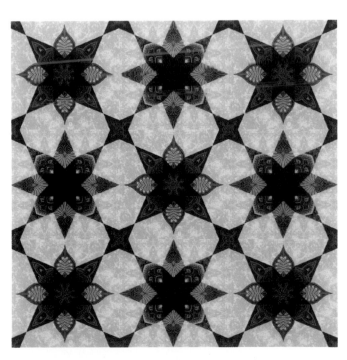

7–51

Signal Light

There is a subtle difference between the hard and soft-edge version of *Signal Light* shown here, but I think the delicate softness of the latter not only enhances the design, but the fabrics that have been used as well.

7–53

7–54

7–55

7–56

Signal Lights

7–57

Springtime Star

The additional color that the soft-edge technique brought to this design made a dramatic difference.

7–58   7–59

7–60   7–61

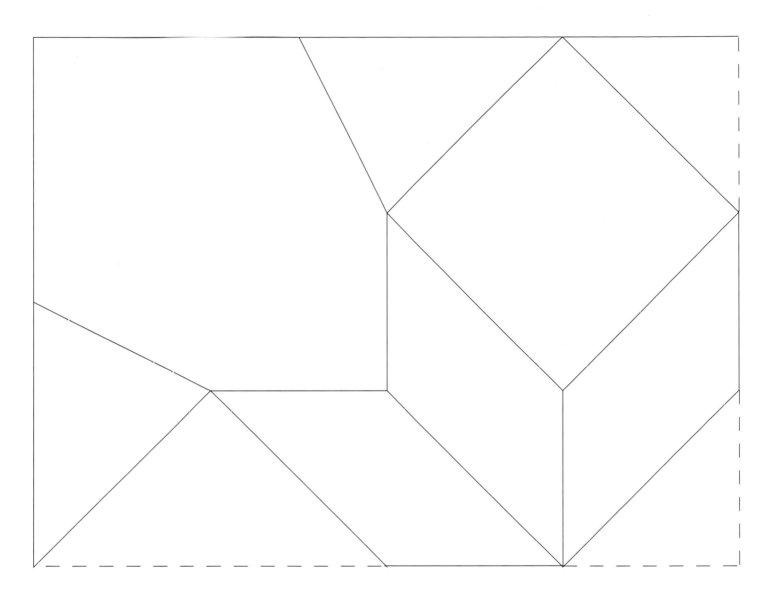

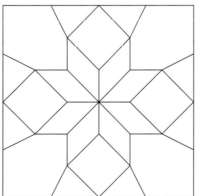

Springtime Star

7–62

RESOURCES

CHECK YOUR LOCAL QUILT SHOP FOR:

- *Border prints, paisleys, and other fabrics with soft-edge capabilities*
- *Mirrors*
- *Transparent template material*
- *Other quilting supplies*
- *Quilter's Disk by Dritz ®*
- *Triangle Tailor's Chalk by Clover*
- *Fray Check ™*
- *Books listed below and in the bibliography*

OTHER JINNY BEYER BOOKS AND PRODUCTS:

Books:
- *Patchwork Patterns, 1979*
- *Quilters Album of Blocks and Borders, 1980*
- *Medallion Quilts, 1982*
- *The Scrap Look, 1985*
- *Patchwork Portfolio, 1989*
- *Color Confidence for Quilters, 1992*

Videos:
- *Palettes for Patchwork, 1987*
- *Mastering Patchwork, 1988*
- *Color Confidence! 1991*

Other:
Portable Palette ®

For products not available from your local quilt store, contact:
JINNY BEYER STUDIO, P.O. Box 488, Great Falls, VA 22066

BIBLIOGRAPHY

Clabburn, Pamela. *The Needleworker's Dictionary.* New York: William Morrow & Co., Inc., 1976.

Beyer, Jinny. *Color Confidence for Quilters.* Gualala, California: The Quilt Digest Press, 1992.

Beyer, Jinny. *Patchwork Patterns.* McLean, Virginia: EPM Publications, Inc., 1979

Beyer, Jinny. *Patchwork Portfolio.* McLean, Virginia: EPM Publications, Inc., 1980

Dillmont, Therese de. *Encyclopedia of Needlework.* Mulhouse, France: T. de Dillmont, 1924.

Other Fine Quilting Books are available from C&T Publishing.
For more information, write for a free catalog from:

C&T Publishing
P.O. Box 1456
Lafayette, CA 94549
1-800-284-1114